Comprehension
Teacher's Guide

Notes and Copymasters
for Introductory Book
and Books 1–4

John Jackman

Published by Collins Educational
An imprint of HarperCollins*Publishers* Ltd
77-85 Fulham Palace Road
London W6 8JB

Browse the complete Collins catalogue at
www.collinseducation.com

First published 1997 as *Collins Primary Comprehension*
Reprinted 1997, 1998, 1999
This edition first published 2002

Reprinted 18 17

ISBN-13   978-0-00-713219-5
ISBN-10   0-00-713219-0

British Library Cataloguing in Publication Data
A catalogue record for this book is available from the British Library.

Editor: Jo Ely
Designer: Neil Adams
Cover photograph: Getty Images © Daniel J Cox

Printed by Martins the Printers Ltd, Berwick

www.harpercollins.co.uk
Visit the book lover's website

Contents

Introduction

Good comprehension skills underpin reading ability and *Focus on Comprehension* has been designed to develop the comprehension skills of all pupils. Each unit of work in *Focus on Comprehension* contains passages to read and questions to answer which have been carefully chosen to excite, interest and enthuse pupils to take their reading and study further.

The hierarchy of skills

Focus on Comprehension provides a structured programme for the teaching of reading comprehension. This equips pupils for:

- reading the lines
- reading between the lines
- reading beyond the lines.

Two very common misconceptions about the teaching of reading comprehension in schools are that, on the one hand, comprehension is a single unitary skill and, on the other hand, that it is a complex of so many skills that it is effectively unmanageable. In avoiding these misconceptions, *Focus on Comprehension* has been founded on the five important comprehension skills described most succinctly by Thomas Barrett in *Reading Today and Tomorrow*:

1. literal comprehension
2. reorganisation
3. inferential and deductive comprehension
4. evaluation
5. appreciation.

The activities in *Focus on Comprehension* focus on each of these five skills and relate to appropriate reading tasks. Broadly speaking, the five skills increase in difficulty from literal comprehension to appreciation and there is a clear progression throughout the five books, enabling pupils to develop all their comprehension skills.

Although no structure can provide complete coverage of teaching about comprehension, *Focus on Comprehension* can help you to effectively plan your classroom programme of work.

Literal comprehension
Literal comprehension focuses on the facts and ideas contained in a reading passage. Appropriate questions in each unit allow pupils to practise the recognition of:

- information explicitly stated, such as detail of characters and settings
- the main ideas
- key sequences of events
- comparisons of characters, times and places
- cause and effect – the reasons for certain things happening.

You can arrange activities so that pupils can answer with the text open in front of them for reference, or with the book closed so that they must recall what is in the text. Recall exercises, significantly more demanding, are an important part of the group of skills which make up effective reading comprehension.

Reorganisation

Reorganisation requires pupils to analyse, or generally organise, information which is explicit. Questions and tasks in each unit require pupils to:

- classify people, things, places, events
- outline and summarise.

Inferential and deductive comprehension

Inferential comprehension entails using the ideas and information explicitly provided in the text, and applying logical processes to them. Deductive comprehension tasks are similar but also require the application of intuition and personal experience to draw conclusions. By implication, the thinking and imagination required by deductive comprehension will go beyond information which is immediately available in the text. The tasks relate to:

- supporting detail which the author has not seen fit to provide
- inferring the main idea, when it is not explicitly provided
- sequencing, most frequently in terms of what might be expected to happen next or what will be the eventual outcome
- providing comparisons between characters, times and places
- relating cause and effect relationships, hypothesising about character motivations and intentions
- interpreting figurative language.

Evaluation

Evaluation implies the making of judgements about a reading passage with outside criteria, including pupils' own evolving personal values and moral code. In the teaching context, it is important to encourage, among other things, the qualities of accuracy and logic, and the ability to assess desirability and probability. These can require the evaluation of:

- reality and fantasy (Could this really have happened?)
- fact and opinion (What is the author's evidence? Is the reader being manipulated?)
- validity (How does the information match up to that from other sources?)
- desirability (Was a character right to act in a given way?)

Appreciation

Appreciation combines all the other dimensions of reading comprehension, dealing as it does with the aesthetic and psychological impact of the text. It calls for pupils to interact with the passage through:

- emotional response to the content in terms of interest, excitement, amusement, fear, and other such emotions
- sympathy for or empathy with characters or situations
- reactions to the author's use of language and imagery.

Statutory and non-statutory guidance

Comprehension is a key to literacy. The teaching of comprehension is of high priority in the primary stages. It also figures importantly in statutory assessment.

Focus on Comprehension has been devised to help support all three English Attainment Targets in the various National Curriculum and National Guideline documents. However, the reading requirements were the clear focus in planning for this programme.

National Curriculum for England and Wales

The National Curriculum (2000) states:

"...pupils read enthusiastically a range of materials and use their knowledge of words, sentences and texts to understand and respond to the meaning. They increase their ability to read challenging and lengthy texts independently. They reflect on the meaning of texts, analysing and discussing them with others."

The general requirements of the National Curriculum for England stipulate:

To develop as effective readers, pupils should be taught to:
- read accurately, fluently and with understanding
- understand and respond to the texts they read
- read, analyse and evaluate a wide range of texts, including literature from the English literary heritage and from other cultures and traditions.

Among the Key Skills stated, of particular significance are:

- Pupils should be taught to consider in detail the quality and depth of what they read.
- They should be encouraged to respond imaginatively to the plot, characters, ideas, vocabulary and organisation of language in literature.
- They should be taught to use inference and deduction.
- Pupils should be taught to evaluate the texts they read.
- Pupils should be taught how to find information in books ... by using organisational devices.
- Pupils should be taught to distinguish between fact and opinion ... consider an argument critically... make succinct notes... note the meaning and use of newly encountered words... re-present information in different forms... use indexes.

The following are the recurring and important themes among the comprehension objectives from the National Literacy Strategy's *Framework for Teaching*:

- evaluating behaviour and relationships of characters
- considering plot sequences
- the organisation of narratives
- awareness of figurative language
- developing and justifying preferences
- locating main points in non-fiction texts
- differentiating fact, fiction, opinion, persuasion.

The accompanying chart shows how the *Focus on Comprehension* programme fits with the comprehension objectives of the National Literacy Strategy.

NLS Text Level objectives	Where objectives are covered in *Focus on Comprehension*, 'Now try these'		
	Book	Unit	Page
Year 1			
(Writing) **Fiction and poetry**			
Write about events in personal experience	Intro	1	5
	Intro	4	11
	1	12	29
Build simple profiles of characters	Intro	7	17
	Intro	10	23
	1	4	11
Use some of the elements of known stories to structure own writing	Intro	4	11
	Intro	6	15
	Intro	7	17
	1	4	11
	1	Prog. A	25
	1	11	27
	1	15	35
	1	17	39
	1	18	41
	1	20	45
	1	Prog. B	47
Non-fiction			
Write and draw simple instructions and labels	Intro	3	9
	Intro	13	29
Write labels for drawings and diagrams	Intro	3	9
	Intro	13	29
	1	5	13
Use simple sentences to describe; and to organise in lists, separate pages, charts	Intro	2	7
	Intro	5	13
	Intro	7	17
	Intro	8	19
	Intro	12	27
	1	2	7
	1	8	19
	1	Prog. A	25
	1	11	27
	1	13	31
	1	18	41
	1	20	45
Write simple recounts	Intro	10	23
	1	5	13
	1	10	23
	1	14	33

NLS Text Level objectives	Where objectives are covered in *Focus on Comprehension*, 'Now try these'		
	Book	**Unit**	**Page**
(Reading)			
Fiction and poetry			
Stories with familiar settings	See Year 2		
Traditional stories and rhymes	See Year 2		
Stories and poems about fantasy worlds	Intro	10	23
Non-fiction			
Signs, labels, captions, lists, instructions	1	12	28
	1	14	32
Information books	See Year 2		
Simple dictionaries	See Year 2		

Year 2			
(Writing)			
Fiction and poetry			
Use story structure to write about own experience in same/similar form	Intro	11	25
	1	7	17
	1	9	21
Write a different story in the same setting	1	16	37
Write character profiles	See Year 1		
Write own nonsense sentences	1	16	37
Non-fiction			
Write simple instructions	Intro	3	9
	Intro	5	13
Organise instructions sequentially	1	5	13
	1	7	17
Write non-chronological reports	Intro	Prog. Test	32
	1	19	43

NLS Text Level objectives	Where objectives are covered in *Focus on Comprehension*, 'Now try these'		
	Book	**Unit**	**Page**
(Reading)			
Fiction and poetry			
Stories/poems with familiar settings	Intro	1	4
	Intro	2	6
	Intro	3	8
	Intro	4	10
	Intro	13	28
	1	5	12
	1	7	16
	1	10	22
	1	11	26
	1	13	30
	1	18	40
Traditional stories	Intro	6	14
	1	10	22
Stories/poems from other cultures	Intro	7	16
	1	9	20
Stories/poems with predictable and patterned language	Intro	8	18
	Intro	12	26
	1	1	4
Poems by significant children's poets	Intro	8	18
	1	3	8
	1	16	36
	1	20	44
Stories by significant children's authors	Intro	Prog. Test	30
	1	15	34
	1	Prog. B	46
Different stories by the same author (Dick King-Smith)	Intro	Prog. Test	30
Riddles, tongue-twisters, humorous verse and stories	Intro	11	24
Non-fiction			
Instructions	Intro	5	12
Dictionaries	Intro	9	20
Explanations			
Information books including non-chronological reports	1	8	18
	1	19	42

NLS Text Level objectives	Where objectives are covered in *Focus on Comprehension*, 'Now try these'		
	Book	**Unit**	**Page**
Year 3			
(Writing) **Fiction and poetry**			
Generate ideas (by brainstorming etc.)	1	13	31
	2	6	15
Develop use of settings in own stories by writing descriptions/story openings	2	3	9 (2)
Stories/poems from other cultures	Intro	7	16
	1	9	20
Collect suitable words/phrases	1	1	5
	1	3	9
	1	5	13
	1	15	35
	1	20	45
	(many examples in each book)		
Plan the main points of a story	1	Progress	47
	4	19	59 (2, 3)
Write portraits of characters	2	17	39
	3	9	28 (2)
	4	1	6 (2)
Write own myth/fable modelled on an original	1	9	21
	2	18	41 (2)
Focus on language for effects	3	6	18 (1)
Write a 1st person account	1	7	17
	1	11	27
	4	5	19 (2b)
Non-fiction			
Make simple records/charts from texts read	1	2	7
	1	6	15
	1	8	19
	1	18	41
	2	Progress	23
	2	10	22
	2	4	11 (1)
	3	5	15
	3	9	28 (3)
	3	15	46
	4	1	6 (4)
	4	5	19 (2a)
	4	11	37 (1)
	4	12	41 (3)
	4	18	56 (2)

NLS Text Level objectives	Where objectives are covered in *Focus on Comprehension*, 'Now try these'		
	Book	**Unit**	**Page**
Write simple non-chronological reports	1	17	39
Write instructions/rules with suitable punctuation	2	19	43 (1, 2)
Write subject-linked letters/notes	1	11	27
	1	20	45
	2	1	5
	3	18	54 (2)
	4	15	47 (1)
	4	20	62 (2)
Recount an event in variety of ways	1	14	33
Summarise the content of a passage	4	Progress (More to think about)	64 (2)
(Reading) **Fiction and poetry**			
Stories with familiar settings	1	7	16
	1	18	40
	1	13	30
	2	19	42
Poems based on observation and the senses	2	10	22
Myths, legends, fables, parables	1	1	4
	1	4	10
	2	18	40
	3	12	37
	3	3	8
	3	20	58
	4	3	10
	4	6	20
	4	10	22
	4	Progress	20
Traditional stories, stories with related themes	1	15	34
	3	19	55
	4	10	29
	4	Progress	32
Oral and performance poetry (different cultures)	2	20	44
Adventure and mystery stories	1	18	40
	2	4	10
Stories by the same author (Dick King-Smith)	2	11	26
	3	4	11
	4	19	57
Humorous poetry, poetry that plays with language, word puzzles, puns, etc.	2	6	14
	2	13	30
	3	17	50
	4	7	22
	4	2	7

NLS Text Level objectives	Where objectives are covered in *Focus on Comprehension*, 'Now try these'		
	Book	**Unit**	**Page**
Non-fiction			
Information books on topics of interest	1	2	16
	1	3	8
	1	6	14
	1	8	18
	1	19	42
	2	2	6
	2	7	16
	2	15	34
	3	15	44
Instructions	See Years 4 and 5		
Letters written for a range of purposes	1	17	38
	3	8	22

Year 4			
(Writing) **Fiction and poetry**			
Write character sketches	1	10	23
	1	15	35
	2	16	37 (1)
	2	Progress	48
	3	16	49 (3)
Write poems on own/imagined experience	1	16	37
Develop use of settings in own writing	3	4	13
	3	17	51 (4)
Write own examples of expressive language (linked to adjectives and similes)	1	19	43
	2	8	19
	2	15	35
Write a story about a dilemma and issues raised for characters concerned	3	11	39 (2)
Write an alternative ending to a known story with appropriate discussion	1	4	11
	2	11	27
	3	4	13 (4)
	3	Progress	33 (1)
	4	13	43 (3a)
	4	17 (More to think about)	53 (3)
Write poems experimenting with different styles/ structure	4	2	9 (4)

NLS Text Level objectives	Where objectives are covered in *Focus on Comprehension*, 'Now try these'		
	Book	Unit	Page
Non-fiction			
Assemble/sequence points of view to plan presentation	3	11	36 (2, 3)
Use writing frames to back up points of view with illustrations and examples	4	11	37 (3)
Write points of view as a letter/report	2	2	7
	2	20	45
	3	2	7 (2)
	3	5	15 (3)
	3	3	10
	3	Progress	64 (2, 3)
	4	8	25 (3)
	4	Progress	34 (1)
	4	19	59 (1)
	4	12	41 (4)
Design a poster/flier	4	8	25 (4)
	4	15	47 (1)
(Reading) **Fiction and poetry**			
Poems based on common themes, e.g. space, school, animals, family	1	1	4
	1	3	8
	1	5	12
	1	16	36
	1	20	44
	2	3	8
	2	16	36
	3	5	14
	4	5	18
Stories/novels about imagined worlds (sci-fi, fantasy, adventures)	2	14	32
	4	16	48
Classic and modern poetry (including different cultures)	2	20	44
	3	17	50
	4	11	35
	4	18	54
Stories/short novels that raise issues, e.g. bullying, bereavement	2	12	28
	2	Progress	46
Stories by the same author	See Year 3		
Stories from other cultures	1	9	20
	2	17	38
	3	9	25
	3	3	8
	3	16	47
	4	4	14
	4	13	42

NLS Text Level objectives	Where objectives are covered in *Focus on Comprehension*, 'Now try these'		
	Book	Unit	Page
Range of poetry in different forms, e.g. haiku, couplets, etc.	3	7	19
	4	7	22
	4	11	35
Non-fiction			
A range of text types from reports and articles in newspapers/magazines	2	Progress	24
	3	Progress	62
	4	15	46
Instructions	3	6	16
Persuasive writing – adverts, circulars, fliers	1	12	28
	4	8	24
Information books linked to other curricular areas	1	14	32
	3	11	34

Year 5			
(Writing) **Fiction and poetry**			
Record ideas/predictions about a book	4	3	13 (3)
	4	6	21 (2,3)
	4	9	28 (2)
Use structures of poems read to write extensions based on them	3	7	21 (3)
	4	2	9 (3)
Write from another character's point of view	3	19	57 (3)
Write about a novel/story – describing/commenting	4	4	16
Non-fiction			
Write recounts based on a subject/topic to various recipients	3	13	41
Make notes for various purposes for use in own speaking/writing	10		4 31 (2)
Write a commentary on an issue justifying views, setting out points, etc.	2	5	13
	3	14	43
(Reading) **Fiction and poetry**			
Novels, stories and poems by significant children's writers	2	8	18
	3	2	6
	3	4	11
	3	18	52
	4	1	4
	4	12	38
	4	16	48
	4	17	51
	4	19	57

NLS Text Level objectives	Where objectives are covered in *Focus on Comprehension*, 'Now try these'		
	Book	**Unit**	**Page**
Traditional stories, myths, legends, fables from a range of cultures	See Year 3		
Longer classic poetry, including narrative poetry	4	18	54
Non-fiction			
Recounts of events, activities, visits	3	2	6
Observational records, news reports, etc.	4	14	44
Instructional texts, rules, recipes, etc.	1	14	32
	2	5	12
Explanations (use contents from other subjects)	3	1	4
	4	20	60

Year 6			
(Writing)			
Non-fiction			
Construct effective arguments logically, developing various points	3	10	31 (1)
(Reading)			
Fiction and poetry			
Classic fiction, poetry and drama by long-established authors	1	15	34
	2	9	20
	3	10	29
	3	13	40
	3	19	55
	4	9	26
	4	10	29
	4	Progress	32
Comparison and study of longer-established stories/ novels from more than one genre	See Year 4		
Non-fiction			
Explanations linked to work from other subjects	1	8	18
	2	3	8
	3	11	34
	4	20	60

Scottish 5–14 Guidelines

The Scottish 5–14 Guidelines state:

- Learning to read accurately and with discrimination becomes increasingly important.
- The importance of meaning should be stressed at all stages.
- [Pupils] should learn to recognise the commoner genre in fiction and non-fiction.
- [Teachers] need to deploy a widening range of techniques such as sequencing, prediction, cloze procedure, evaluating the text, [and] making deductions.

The teacher can focus on texts... during and after reading by:

- providing questions which ask for literal, inferential and evaluative responses
- asking [pupils] to demonstrate understanding by doing or speaking
- asking...[pupils]...to use the text as a model for their own writing.

Northern Ireland Curriculum

The Northern Ireland Curriculum states:

Pupils should develop the ability to read, understand and engage with various types of text for enjoyment and learning...and among their reading activities, pupils should have opportunities for:

- justifying their responses logically, by inference, deduction and reference to the evidence within the text
- paying attention to what is written and how it is expressed
- extending their capacity for sympathy and empathy
- predicting what may happen or considering what might have happened had circumstances been different.

Welsh Curriculum

The Welsh Curriculum states:

[Pupils] should read widely, for enjoyment and information, through progressively more challenging and demanding texts, and they should be taught to reflect upon and evaluate their reading.

Pupils should be taught to:

- read with increasing fluency, accuracy, understanding and enjoyment
- use inference, deduction and prediction to evaluate the texts they read
- adopt appropriate strategies for a specified task by identifying the precise information that they wish to know
- adopt appropriate strategies for a specified task by distinguishing between fact and opinion.

Using Focus on Comprehension

Focus on Comprehension is made up of units which have been devised in order to develop from the beginning the range of the five important comprehension skills. Skill requirements become increasingly sophisticated as the course progresses.

Each book, except the Introductory book, contains 20 carefully structured units, each of which include one or more passages of text. In addition, each book contains two Progress Units designed to evaluate pupils' skill development and progress in terms of the end of key stage assessment. The Introductory book contains 13 teaching units and one Progress Unit. Each unit in all five books follows the same structure. This both sets up an expectation in the children and teacher, and provides for a balanced diet of reading comprehension exercises.

Developing comprehension skills

Every unit of work is organised around three headings: *Do you remember?*, *More to think about* and *Now try these*.

Do you remember?
Reading the lines
- literal comprehension (easier recognition and recall activities)

More to think about
Reading between the lines
- literal comprehension (more challenging recognition and recall activities)
- reorganisation (classifying; summarising and synthesising)
- inferential and deductive comprehension (supporting detail; the main idea; sequencing; comparison of characters, settings; cause and effect; character traits; prediction)

Now try these
Reading beyond the lines
- evaluation (reality/fantasy; fact/opinion; validity; appropriateness; acceptability)
- appreciation (emotional response; empathy with characters or incidents; understanding of, and reactions to, use of language and imagery)

Classroom management and progression

The course has been structured and arranged to be straightforward and easy to use. If you feel it is appropriate, you can use the material in the context of whole-class teaching. Equally, this material is flexible and can be used by individuals or small groups at their own pace.

In the context of whole-class teaching, it is suggested that the first part of each lesson should be to read aloud the passage of text. Discussion of the stimulus material, including the illustrations, would follow, with selected questions being tackled by you and the class together. The questions for pupils allow for group work, and have been prepared to ensure a minimum of teacher intervention. This will enable you to spend time with groups as they undertake different sections of the work.

The *Do you remember?* questions, which require a literal response to the text, are likely to be the least challenging, and have been written to be accessible to the majority of pupils. The *More to think about* questions are more difficult and the *Now try these* questions are more demanding still.

A wide range of question forms have been built into the course. Details of the questions are listed in the following teacher's notes for each unit and, where appropriate, the questions themselves have been given for your easier reference. It is helpful if you point out the requirements of the questions in each unit before pupils begin writing.

A range of genre

Each unit begins with a passage which has been carefully selected to represent the range of genre required by the National Curricula of England, Wales and Northern Ireland, and referred to in the Scottish 5–14 guidelines.

Modern/established writers

Introductory Book
Hiding, by Shirley Hughes; *Our Dog*, by Helen Oxenbury; *Owl in the House*, by Gregory Evans; *Judy and the Martian*, by Penelope Lively; *Two Legs or Four?*, by Dick King-Smith

Book 1
Gumdrop has a Birthday, by Val Biro; *The Golly Sisters Go West*, by Betsy Byers; *Hot Dog Harris*, by Rose Impey; *The Dragon's Cold*, by John Talbot; *The Owl Who Was Afraid of the Dark*, by Jill Tomlinson; *Crash!* (a picture book)

Book 2
Tim the Trumpet, by Elizabeth Beresford; *The Swoose*, by Dick King-Smith; *Dr Xargle's Book of Earthlets*, by Jeanne Willis; *Mrs Wobble the Waitress*, by Allan and Janet Ahlberg; *Angry Arthur*, by Hiawyn Oram; *The Dragon's Egg*, by R.L. Green; *Three Girls*, by Michael Rosen

Book 3
The Chicken Gave it to Me, by Anne Fine; *The Invisible Dog*, by Dick King-Smith; *The Big Match*, by Rob Childs; *Snakes and Ladders*, by Michael Morpurgo; *The Snow Spider*, by Jenny Nimmo

Book 4
The TV Kid, by Betsy Byers; *The BFG*, by Roald Dahl; *Trouble Half-Way*, by Jan Mark; *The Phantom Tollbooth*, by Norton Juster; *Martin's Mice*, by Dick King-Smith

Long established fiction

Book 1
The Tale of Peter Rabbit, by Beatrix Potter

Book 2
The Wind in the Willows, by Kenneth Grahame

Book 3
The Borrowers, by Mary Norton; *Robinson Crusoe*, by Daniel Defoe; *Black Beauty*, by Anna Sewell

Book 4
Gulliver's Travels, by Jonathan Swift; *The Little Match Girl*, by Hans Christian Anderson; *The Railway Children*, by E. Nesbit

Poetry (modern and classic)

Introductory Book
When I Was One, by A.A. Milne; *When the Wind Blows*, by John Foster; *A Very Busy Day*, by Martin Skelton and David Playfoot

Book 1
The Cow, by Robert Louis Stevenson; *Big Bulgy Fat Slugs*, by Berlie Doherty; *Roger the Dog*, by Ted Hughes; *Now Isn't It Amazing*, by Max Fatchen; *Caterpillars*, by Eric Slater

Poetry (modern and classic) *continued*

Book 2
Tadpoles, by Stanley Cook; *I Love Our Orange Tent*, by Berlie Doherty; *Magic*, by Shel Silverstein; *Bus Route*, by David Harmer; *What is...the Sun?*, by Wes Magee; *My Hair*, by Bertie Thomson

Book 3
The Donkey, Anon; *The Shark*, by Lord Alfred Douglas; *From a Railway Carriage*, by Robert Louis Stevenson

Book 4
Colonel Fazackerley, by Charles Causley; *Hiawatha's Childhood*, H.W. Longfellow; *A Smuggler's Song*, by Rudyard Kipling; *Crack-a-Dawn*, by Brian Morse; *Winter Morning*, by Ogden Nash; *Winter in a Wheelchair*, by Emma Barnes

Texts from other cultures

Introductory Book
Hippo and Monkey

Book 1
Thunder and Lightning

Book 2
A Day when Frogs wear Shoes, by Ann Kameron; *Kob Antelope*, Anon

Book 3
The Two Brothers; *Sedna, the Great Inuit Goddess*

Book 4
The Discontented Fish; *The King, Compere Lapin and Compere Tig*; *Why Bats Fly at Night*

Myths, legends, traditional stories

Introductory Book
Gingerbread Man

Book 1
The Lion and the Mouse, Aesop's fable; *The Three Billy Goats Gruff*

Book 2
The Eagle and the Turtle, Aesop's fable; *Basilisks*

Book 3
A Clever Way to Catch a Thief; *Ou and Ouch*; *The Lonely Boy*

Book 4
The Trojan War, *Shen Nung*

Information sources

Introductory Book
Looking After Your Bike (reference); *Looking at a Dictionary* (dictionary page); *Monkey Business* (newspaper article)

Book 1
An Ant's Nest (information book); *Looking at Books* (covers); *Working on a Farm* (picture sequence); *Gran's New House* (letter); *Fun on Bikes* (poster); *Funny Feeders* (reference); *Lost in the Zoo* (map)

Assessment and record keeping

Assessment looms large in all our lives. *Focus on Comprehension* provides
support in a simple and direct way:

There are two Progress Units within each book, except the Introductory book
which has one. These allow you to assess pupils' development and progress in
terms of the end of key stage assessment.

Recording pupils' progress is an important aspect of educational good practice.
To enable the efficient classroom management of this, a record form has been
given on the following page. This will allow you to keep an eye on individual
pupils' progress and achievement as well as keeping a more generalised
record for the class as a whole.

Focus on Comprehension: Class Record

Book _____ Class _____ Year _____

It is suggested that you give a brief indication of pupils' progress for each unit:
/ = attempted; X = completed satisfactorily

Names	Units																					
	1	2	3	4	5	6	7	8	9	10	A	11	12	13	14	15	16	17	18	19	20	B

Focus on Comprehension: Individual Record

Name _____ Book _____ Class _____ Year _____

Unit	Comment	Date
1		
2		
3		
4		
5		
6		
7		
8		
9		
10		
Progress Unit A		
11		
12		
13		
14		
15		
16		
17		
18		
19		
20		
Progress Unit B		

Teacher's notes and answers

Introductory Book

Scope and sequence of skills

Unit	Title	Page	Do you remember? *Reading the lines*	More to think about *Reading between the lines*	Now try these *Reading beyond the lines*
1	**Hiding** *Modern fiction*	4	cloze from passage	selecting true sentences	deductive answering in sentences
2	**The Picnic** *Modern fiction*	6	selecting correct answers	literal and deductive answers in sentences	empathy
3	**Our Dog** *Modern fiction*	8	cloze selected from words offered	assessing true or not true	ordering instructions
4	**Owl in the House** *Modern fiction*	10	word selection	selecting true sentences	story completion; character empathy
5	**Looking After Your Bike** *Reference*	12	selecting true sentences	literal answering in sentences	empathy
6	**Gingerbread Man** *Traditional story*	14	word selection	sequencing events	character empathy
7	**Hippo and Monkey** *Nigerian folk tale*	16	assessing yes or no	classifying	story completion; empathy
8	**When I Was One** *Classic poem*	18	cloze from picture	selecting rhyming words	emotional empathy
9	**Looking at a Dictionary** *Dictionary page*	20	literal answering	literal answering	referencing
10	**Judy and the Martian** *Modern fiction*	22	selecting correct sentence endings	literal answering in sentences	character empathy and interpreting language
11	**Monkey Business** *Newspaper article*	24	word selection	literal and deductive answering in sentences	character empathy

Introductory Book

Unit 1 Hiding

Do you remember?
cloze from passage

1. Where is the boy hiding?
   The boy is hiding under the bush.
2. Where is the girl hiding?
   The girl is hiding under the umbrella.
3. Which animals are hiding in their shells?
   Tortoises are hiding in their shells.
4. Who is hiding behind a newspaper?
   Dad is hiding behind a newspaper.

More to think about
selecting true sentences

The following sentences should have been selected:
Dad is hiding behind his newspaper.
Tortoises hide in their shells.
The baby thinks you can't see him.

Now try these
deductive answering in sentences

Pupils should write a sentence in their own words to answer each question.
1. Why do you think Dad hides behind his newspaper?
   Dad hides behind his newspaper to pretend he isn't there.
   [check]
2. Why does the baby think you can't see him when he hides his eyes?
   The baby thinks you can't see him when he hides his eyes because he can't see you!
3. Where is your favourite hiding place?
   My favourite hiding place is...

Unit 2 The Picnic

Do you remember?
selecting correct answers

Choose a word from the box to answer each question.
1. What was the uncle's name? *Ben*
2. Who was the oldest person at the picnic? *Gran*
3. How many people were there? *five*
4. What might the children climb? *trees*
5. What did Mum ask the children to get from the car?
   chairs

More to think about
literal and deductive answering in sentences

Pupils should write a sentence in their own words to answer each question.
1. What did Gran grumble about?
   Gran grumbled that her legs were stiff from sitting in the car.
2. Why did the children think it was a good place for a picnic?
   The children thought it was a good place for a picnic because there were trees to climb.
3. How do we know it hadn't been raining?
   We know it hadn't been raining because the grass was dry.
4. Why couldn't they see the stream from the picnic spot?
   The stream couldn't be seen because it was behind the bushes.
5. Why do you think Tim said, "But, Mum"?
   Tim said "But, Mum," because he wanted to run off and play.

Now try these
empathy

1. Make a list of the things that you need to take on a picnic.
   Food, drink, chairs, blanket, tablecloth, cutlery
2. Write about what you think the children did after they had eaten their picnic.
   (Children's own answer)
Note: *Pupils need to use empathy to 'think themselves into' a particular situation.*

Unit 3 Our Dog

Do you remember?
cloze selected from words offered

1. The dog has a walk every *day*.
2. One day she jumped in a *smelly* pond.
3. She also rolled in the *mud*.
4. They took the dog home and gave her a *bath*.

More to think about
assessing true or not true

1. The dog has a walk once a week. *not true*
2. She barks when she wants a walk. *not true*
3. The dog likes water. *true*
4. Sometimes she gets herself muddy. *true*
5. She has a bath in the kitchen. *not true*
6. The dog sits quietly in the bath. *not true*

Now try these
ordering instructions
The instructions for bathing the dog are in the wrong order.
Write them in the right order.
Fill the bath with warm water.
Lift the dog into the water.
Splash the water onto the dog's coat.
Rub shampoo into her wet coat.
Rinse off all the soap.
Dry her with a towel.
Draw a picture of the dog in the bath.
Make up a name for the dog. (Children's own answer)
Under the picture write the dog's name.

Unit 4 Owl in the House

Do you remember?
word selection
1. A sudden gust of *wind* made owl lose his balance.
2. He *tumbled* into the chimney.
3. He felt *frightened*.
4. In the hall, Owl *spread* his wings.
5. The *house* was locked up tight.

More to think about
selecting true sentences
The following sentences should have been selected:
Owl was quite young.
It was a stormy night.
His feathers got covered in soot.
Owl was trapped in the house.

Now try these
story completion; character empathy
Pupils should write some sentences in their own words to answer each question.
1. What do you think happened next?
   Write your own ending. (Children's own answer)
2. Pretend that you are trapped somewhere.
   Write some sentences about where you are and how you feel. (Children's own answer)
Note: *Both assignments call for empathy with the situation, and can provide fruitful starting points for discussion and imaginative exploration prior to the commencement of written work.*

Unit 5 Looking After Your Bike

Do you remember?
selecting true sentences
The following sentences should have been selected:
A bike is a machine.
Bikes get rusty if they are left out in the rain.
You need to keep your bike well oiled.
Every bike rider should wear a helmet.

More to think about
literal answering in sentences
Pupils should write a sentence in their own words to answer each question.
1. Why do you need to keep your bike dry?
   Your bike needs to be kept dry so it won't get rusty.
2. Why are brakes important?
   Brakes are very important for safety.

3. How can you tell if your seat is the correct height?
   The seat is the correct height if both your feet can touch the ground when you sit on it.
4. Which parts of your bike need to be oiled?
   The chain, pedals and levers need oiling.
5. What should you always wear when riding your bike?
   You should always wear a helmet when riding your bike.

Now try these
empathy
1. Pretend it is your birthday. You have been given a new bike. Describe what it is like. *(Children's own answer)*
2. Make a list of the good things about having a bike.
   It's fun to ride. You can ride to school. You feel grown up.
3. Write the main safety rules for bike riders.
   1. Wear a helmet. 2. Check the brakes. 3. Check air in tyres. 4. Keep chain, pedals and levers oiled. 5. Seat at correct height.
Note: *As a group encourage pupils to consider safety rules for bike riders and discuss why the rules are in place.*

Unit 6 Gingerbread Man

Do you remember?
word selection
1. The gingerbread man jumped from the *oven*.
2. First he ran past the *cat*.
3. On he ran past the *bird*.
4. When he reached the *lake* he stopped.
5. A *fox* said he would help.

More to think about
sequencing events
The sentences should be ordered as follows:
Gran made a gingerbread man.
The gingerbread man jumped from the oven.
He ran past the cat.
The bird tried to stop the gingerbread man.
He came to the lake.

Now try these
character empathy
Pupils should write some sentences in their own words to answer each question.
1. Pretend you are the gingerbread man.
   Write about how you feel when you come to the lake. (Children's own answer)
2. Write the reasons why you think the gingerbread man can't cross the lake by himself.
   He can't swim. He will melt in the water. He's afraid of water. He's too small.
3. Write your own ending for the story. Try to make it a surprise. *(Children's own answer)*
Note: *Pupils will need to use empathy to 'think themselves into' this situation and explore their feelings. Encourage the children to share their ideas about how the story might end.*

Unit 7 Hippo and Monkey

Do you remember?
assessing yes or no

1. Monkey thought he was the strongest animal in the world. *no*
2. Monkey played a trick on Hippo. *yes*
3. Hippo liked to sit in the pool all day. *yes*
4. All the animals helped Monkey to pull the rope. *no*
5. While Hippo pulled, Monkey ate bananas. *yes*

More to think about
classifying

Pupils are asked to sort a group of words into two lists.

Words that describe Monkey	Words that describe Hippo
brown	grey
clever	huge
small	fat
thin	moody
	grumpy

Now try these
story completion; empathy

1. Write the end of the story in your own words.
   (Children's own answer)
2. Who was more clever, Hippo or Monkey? Say why you think this.
   Monkey fooled Hippo. Monkey made Hippo think he was stronger.

Note: *This question requires pupils to draw inferences from the text.*

Unit 8 When I Was One

Do you remember?
cloze from picture

1. There are six candles on the *cake.*
2. The *cat* is under the table.
3. The boy hasn't opened his *presents* yet.
4. Four *children/friends* have come to his party.
5. There are bunches of *balloons* on the wall.

More to think about
selecting rhyming words

Pupils are asked to find matching rhyming words from the poem.

1. a) one...*begun*   b) two...*new*   c) three...*me*
   d) four...*more*   e) five...*alive*

Pupils are asked to find their own words that rhyme with the following:

2. a) one b) two c) three

Now try these
emotional empathy

1. Write a list of the five things you like best about birthdays.
   (Children's own answer)
2. Write a list of three things you don't like about birthdays.
   (Children's own answer)

Note: *This is an opportunity for pupils to explore their own feelings about birthdays.*

Unit 9 Looking at a Dictionary

Do you remember?
literal answering

1. How many words begin with e?
   Eight words begin with e.
2. How many words begin with f?
   Six words begin with f.
3. Which is the first word that begins with e?
   Ever is the first word that begins with e.
4. Which is the last word that begins with f?
   Fall is the last word that begins with f.

More to think about
literal answering

Pupils should write a sentence in their own words to answer each question.

1. What are the two things we can use a dictionary for?
   Dictionaries tell us what words mean and help us spell words.
2. *The children are asked to copy the meanings of these words.*
   a) excellent – very, very good
   b) expect – to think something will happen
   c) explode – to blow up
   d) fact – something that is true
   e) factory – a building where things are made
   f) fall – to drop down
3. Which words have two different meanings?
   Examination, face and fail have two different meanings.
4. Which word has three different meanings?
   Fair has three different meanings.

Now try these
referencing

The children are asked to draw a line to match the words and their meanings.

1.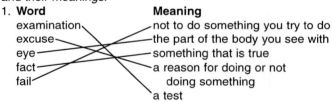

Word

examination
excuse
eye
fact
fail

Meaning

not to do something you try to do
the part of the body you see with
something that is true
a reason for doing or not doing something
a test

The children are asked to write a meaning for each of the words and then to check their definitions in a dictionary.

2. a) acorn   *a nut which grows on an oak tree*
   b) blow   *when the wind blows the air moves faster*
   when you blow you send out a stream of air from your mouth
   a hard hit
   c) canal   *a narrow stretch of water for boats to travel along*
   d) dislike   *someone or something you do not like*
   e) enjoy   *something you like doing very much*
   f) free   *someone who is free can go where they want*
   if something is free it does not cost anything

[These definitions are based on those found in the Collins Junior Dictionary.]

Note: *This activity encourages children to think about definitions of words. They may need support in checking their definitions in a dictionary.*

Unit 10 Judy and the Martian

Do you remember?
selecting correct sentence endings

1. The rocket landed in a *car park*.
2. The Martian had *green skin*.
3. He was *327 years old*.
4. When it rained he *went into the supermarket*.

More to think about
literal answering in sentences

Pupils should write a sentence in their own words to answer each question.

1. Why did the rocket land in the car park?
   The rocket landed in the car park because the engine had failed.
2. What did the Martian look like?
   The Martian had webbed feet, green skin and eyes on the ends of horns like a snail.
3. When did the Martian pass his driving test?
   The Martian passed his driving test the week before.
4. Why did he scuttle behind a rubbish bin?
   He scuttled behind a rubbish bin because a car hooted.
5. How did the Martian get into the supermarket?
   The Martian got into the supermarket through the sliding door at the back which had been left open a little.

Now try these
character empathy and interpreting language

Pupils should write some sentences in their own words to answer each question.

1. Draw a picture of the Martian standing next to his rocket in the car park. Write some sentences about how he feels in this strange new world. *(Children's own answer)*
   Note: *This activity seeks to establish empathy with the Martian.*
2. Which word in the story means:
   a) broken down *failed*
   b) an opening like a small door *hatch*
   c) very, very *extremely*
   d) ran with little steps *scuttled*
   e) to twist and turn *wriggle*

Unit 11 Monkey Business

Do you remember?
word selection

1. The monkeys escaped from a *lorry*.
2. It was taking them to a *zoo*.
3. They got out through the *door*.
4. *Most* of the car drivers thought it was funny.
5. The police inspector called them *cheeky chimps*.

More to think about
literal and deductive answering in sentences

Pupils should write a sentence in their own words to answer each question.

1. Where were the chimps being taken?
   The chimps were being taken to Burwell Zoo.
2. Do you think the chimps were pleased to be out of the lorry? Why?
   I think the chimps thought it was great fun to be out of the lorry because they didn't like being stuck in the lorry.
3. How did the monkeys get out of the lorry?
   The chimps got out of the lorry by lifting the latch on the door.
4. Why were some of the drivers cross?
   Some of the drivers were cross because the chimps caused a traffic jam.

Now try these
character empathy

1. Think of an animal you would like to be. Write some sentences to say why.
2. Pretend that you are a rabbit living in a hutch all day. You can see children playing in the garden. Write about how you might feel. *(Children's own answer)*
Note: *Pupils will need to use empathy to 'think themselves into' the animals and explore their feelings. Although not essential, it would be helpful to discuss the questions before the pupils write the answers. Encourage children to write answers in sentences, with correct punctuation.*

Unit 12 When the Wind Blows

Do you remember?
cloze selected from words offered

Pupils should select the correct word from a box.

1. When the wind blows scarves flutter.
2. When the wind blows leaves mutter.
3. When the wind blows papers scatter.
4. When the wind blows dustbins clatter.

More to think about
assessing 'always', 'sometimes', 'never'

1. On windy days chimneys get blown off roofs. *sometimes*
2. On windy days it is freezing cold going to school. *sometimes*
3. On windy days the sun shines. *sometimes*
4. On windy days the air doesn't move. *never*
5. On windy days ships get wrecked. *sometimes*
6. On windy days flags flap in the breeze. *always*

Now try these
lists – assessing and evaluating

1. Imagine it is a windy day. Make two lists in your book:
   Things I like about windy days
   Things I dislike about windy days *(Children's own answer)*
2. What is your favourite weather? Say why you like it best. *(Children's own answer)*
Note: *These assignments call for empathy with the situation and can provide starting points for discussion and imaginative written work.*

Unit 13 A Very Busy Day

Do you remember?
selecting true sentences

The following sentences should have been selected:
Our hair is growing all the time.
We must eat food to live.
All the bones in our bodies make our skeletons.
Our brains are very important.

Introductory Book

More to think about
literal answering in sentences

*Pupils should write a sentence in their own words to answer
each question.*
1. What do we use our teeth for?
   Our teeth are used to cut and chew food.
2. What does our nose do?
   Our nose smells smells.
3. What stops germs getting inside us?
   Our skin stops germs getting inside us.
4. How are our bones moved?
   Our muscles move our bones.
5. What pumps the blood around our bodies?
   The heart pumps the blood around our bodies.

Now try these
simple deduction

1. Draw a picture of yourself. Write these labels on
   the picture:
   head knee ankle elbow shoulder neck chest
2. Make a list of five rules to help you keep healthy.
   *1. Warm clothes in winter. 2. Eat properly. 3. Drink milk.
   4. Don't eat lots of sweets. 5. Play sports.*

Note: *The children may need help to think of situations in
order to consider how best they might stay healthy.*

Progress Unit Two Legs or Four?

Do you remember?
cloze selected from answers given

Score: 1 mark for each correct answer (maximum 4 marks)

*Pupils should select the correct answer from two possible
choices.*
1. What new pet did the family have?
   b) They had a puppy.
2. Who wanted the new pet to be called Ben?
   b) Ben wanted it called Ben.
3. How did the puppy behave?
   a) It was a good puppy.
4. Did the puppy mess on the carpets?
   b) No, the puppy never messed on the carpets.

More to think about
deductive answering in sentences

*Score: 2 marks for each sentence, depending on content and
punctuation(maximum 10 marks).*

*Pupils should write a sentence in their own words to answer
each question.*
1. Why was it useful to have the boy and the puppy with the
   same name?
   *It was useful for the boy and puppy to have the same
   name because the same words served for both of them.*
2. What did the puppy do when the boy laughed?
   When the boy laughed the puppy barked.

3. What did the puppy do when the boy lost his temper?
   When the boy lost his temper the puppy growled.
4. Why do you think the puppy took to copying everything
   the boy did?
   (Children's own answer)
5. Name one of the problems that came from both being
   called Ben.
   *One of the problems of them both being called Ben was
   that it could cause confusion when talking about one
   of them.*

Now try these
emotional response and interpreting language

*Score: Question 1, award up to 10 marks, depending on the
extent the child is empathising with the situation, as well
as taking account of the content and punctuation.
Question 2, 1 mark for each correct answer (maximum
16 marks).*

1. Pretend that you have just been given a new pet. Draw a
   picture of it. Write about how you feel and how you will
   look after it.
Note: *Pupils will need to use empathy to 'think themselves
into' the situation and explore their feelings.*
2. *The following links between words with similar meanings
   should be made:*
   Find words in the story that mean:
   a) becoming mixed up *confusing*
   b) shouting *yelling*
   c) giving an order *ordered*
   d) the same amount *equally*
   e) crossly *angrily*
   f) rolling head-over-heels *turning somersaults*

Indicative scores for National Curriculum

Below level 2	Level 2	Level 3
0-7	8-24	25-30

Indicative scores for 5–14 Guidelines

Level A	Level B	Level C
0-8	9-26	27-30

FOCUS

on Comprehension

Book 1

Scope and sequence of skills

Unit	Title	Page	Do you remember? *Reading the lines*	More to think about *Reading between the lines*	Now try these *Reading beyond the lines*
1	**Caterpillars** *Modern poem*	4	word selection	literal and deductive answering in sentences	vocabulary work; simple imagery
2	**Working on a Farm** *Reading pictures*	6	word selection	sentence completion; literal answers	empathy – likes/dislikes
3	**The Cow** *Classic poem*	8	selecting true sentences	selecting sentence endings	evaluating statements; vocabulary work
4	**The Three Billy Goats Gruff** *Traditional story*	10	cloze from passage	assessing true/false/ can't tell	character empathy; story completion
5	**Now Isn't It Amazing?** *Modern poem/non-fiction*	12	word selection	sentence sequencing	vocabulary work; incident empathy
6	**Looking at Books** *Book covers*	14	cloze	deductive answering	referencing
7	**Gumdrop has a Birthday** *Modern fiction*	16	selecting correct sentences	sequencing a recipe; selecting/ordering phrases	evaluating statements; character empathy
8	**An Ants' Nest** *Information book extract*	18	cloze from passage	deductive answering in sentences; collating factual statements	lists - assessing and evaluating
9	**Thunder and Lightning** *Text from other cultures*	20	selecting true sentences incident empathy	sentence sequencing	vocabulary work;

Book 1

Unit 1 Caterpillars

Do you remember?
word selection

Pupils should select the correct ending from two possible choices.
1. The caterpillars look like *clowns*.
2. They are clinging to twigs with their *feet*.
3. They are looking for something to *eat*.
4. Caterpillars eat mostly *leaves*.
5. *Green* is the most usual colour of caterpillars.

More to think about
literal and deductive answering in sentences

Pupils should write a sentence in their own words to answer each question.
1. In what way are some caterpillars like circus clowns?
   Caterpillars are painted bright like circus clowns.
2. Are all caterpillars smooth to touch?
   Not all caterpillars are smooth to touch.
   [The pupils might refer to the bristles some caterpillars have.]
3. What different sorts of patterns do caterpillars have on their bodies?
   Some caterpillars have spots and some have patches like polka dots.

4. What is the most common colour of caterpillars?
   Green is the most common colour of caterpillars.
5. Is it easier to spot a green or a red caterpillar on a green leaf?
   It is easier to spot a red caterpillar on a green leaf.
6. Why is it better for caterpillars if they are not easy to find?
   If caterpillars are less easy to find they are more protected from danger/less likely to be attacked.

Now try these
vocabulary work; simple imagery

1. Find a word in the poem that rhymes with:
   a) down *clown* b) feet *eat* c) spots *dots*
   d) blue *chew*
2. *Pupils should find words in the poem that rhyme with each of those given. The first one has been done for pupils, as an example.*
   clinging = holding; *chewing = munching;*
   looking = searching; dots = spots; tiny = small
3. The poet says some caterpillars look like clowns. Make a list of anything else they remind you of.
   Notes: *Children's answers should reflect colour, size or movement and other behavioural characteristics (such as voracious appetite) of the caterpillar.*

Unit 2 Working on a Farm

Do you remember?
word selection

1. The *farmer* is Mr Lindsay.
2. In picture 1 the farmer is *ploughing*.
3. After ploughing, he *rakes* the ground.
4. The ground is now ready for sowing the *seed*.
5. The seed needs *rain* to help it grow.

More to think about
sentence completion; literal answers

Pupils should answer in sentences. The beginnings of the first three sentences have been given, to help them.

1. Why does Farmer Lindsay need to plough the ground?
   The ground is ploughed so that it can be made ready for sowing.
2. Why are the birds close by while the farmer is ploughing?
   The birds are looking for worms and insects in the soil.
3. Does he sow the seed before or after raking?
   He sows the seed after raking.
4. What sort of weather helps the seed to grow?
   Warm and rainy weather helps the seed to grow best.
5. What job is being done in picture 4?
   In picture 4 the farmer is harvesting.
6. Which season does picture 4 show?
   Picture 4 shows a summer scene.

Now try these
empathy – likes/dislikes

Notes: *Pupils are asked to imagine that they are a farmer and write what they like and dislike about being a farmer in their own words. Their likes may include things such as: working outside in the sunshine; being with animals; driving tractors. Their dislikes may include: working outside in the rain/cold; cleaning out animals. Encourage consideration of the pros and cons.*

Unit 3 The Cow

Do you remember?
selecting true sentences

The following sentences should have been selected:
The cow is red and white.
She likes to eat meadow flowers.
When it rains she gets wet.
Her milk is made into cream.

More to think about
selecting sentence endings

Pupils should select the correct ending from three possible choices.

1. The cow in the poem *a) is friendly*
2. Her coat is *b) red and white*
3. Some of her milk is made into *c) cream*
4. She wanders about *b) making contented sounds*
5. When it rains *a) she gets wet*

Now try these
evaluating statements; vocabulary work

1. a) How do we know the poet probably owns the cow?
      The poet probably owns the cow as he uses her cream.
   b) Does he say he loves her with all his heart just because of the cream she gives? What other reasons might he have?
      Pupils may refer here to the friendliness of the cow and other character traits.
   c) What word does the poet use to make you know he likes the outdoor life?
      pleasant
2. Find these words in the poem. Write other words that mean the same.
   a) with all my heart, *for example: a lot, deeply, enormously*
   b) with all her might, *for example: to the best of her ability*
   c) pleasant, *for example: enjoyable, agreeable*

Unit 4 The Three Billy Goats Gruff

Do you remember?
cloze from passage

1. There were *three* billy goats.
2. They had eaten all the *leaves*.
3. Now they were feeling very *hungry*.
4. There were more leaves across the *stream*.
5. An ugly old *troll* lived under the bridge.

More to think about
Assessing true/false/can't tell

1. There were three goats. *true*
2. The goats were sisters. *false (this requires pupils to know billy goats are male, so 'can't tell' is also acceptable)*
3. They liked beech leaves more than ash leaves. *can't tell*
4. The troll was young. *false*
5. Little Billy Goat Gruff was very hungry. *true*
6. He said he wasn't afraid of the troll. *true*

Now try these
character empathy; story completion

1. In your book write some sentences about the troll. Write about what he was like, and why you think he came to live under the bridge.
   Notes: *Based on the illustration as well as the text, the pupil should describe the personality and physical appearance of the troll, and speculate as to why the troll*

might choose to live under the bridge, for example because he had been evicted from his own home; because it is a good hunting spot; because he likes water.

2. Make up <u>your own</u> ending for this well-known story.
   Notes: *Encourage an imaginative response; don't accept the traditional tossing of the troll into the stream by Big Billy Goat Gruff.*

Unit 5 Now Isn't It Amazing?

Do you remember?
cloze selected from words offered

Pupils should select the correct ending from two possible choices.

1. Seeds grow into *flowers.*
2. Grubs turn into *butterflies.*
3. Rainbows come from sun and *showers.*
4. Bees make *honey.*
5. Birds grow from *eggs.*

More to think about
sentence sequencing

The sentences should be sequenced in this order:
The seed falls onto the ground.
The young plant begins to shoot.
Rain keeps it damp and the sun keeps it warm.
It has a beautiful red flower in the summer.

Now try these
vocabulary work; incident empathy

1. Find a word in the poem that rhymes with:
   a) flowers *showers*   b) amazing *lazing*
   Now think of other words that rhyme with each of these words.
   Notes: *Note that different spelling patterns are equally acceptable, and if not offered can be a useful point for discussion and extension work, for example*
   a) *powers towers*   b) *gazing grazing*
      hours ours   *praising raising phasing*
2. What is the most amazing thing you have ever seen or heard about? Say why you think it is so special.
   Notes: *Pupils need to use empathy to 'think themselves into' a particular incident, and explore their feelings about it.*

Unit 6 Looking at Books

Do you remember?
cloze

1. The title of the book is *Keeping Small Animals.*
2. The author of the book is called *James Matthews.*
3. An author is the person who *writes* the words.
4. The name of the illustrator of the book is *Sarah Richards.*
5. An illustrator is the person who *draws* the pictures.

More to think about
deductive answering

1. Which is the story book?   *1*
2. In which book could I check the meaning of a word?   *4*
3. Which book did Hilary Frost write?   *3*
4. In which book might I find facts about rabbits?   *2*
5. Which book will help me check the spelling of a word?   *4*
6. Which book might tell me about the River Amazon?   *3*

7. Which of the books was written by Kenneth Grahame?   *1*
8. In which *two* books might I discover more about where alligators live?   *2 and 3*

Now try these
referencing

Write the title and author of one of each of these types of books that you can find in your classroom.
A book that:
1. tells you about birds
2. has a story
3. helps you with spelling words
4. has lots of pictures
5. is about another country
6. is your favourite
   Notes: *This activity lends itself to early discussions on the merits of individual books, and gives an opportunity for the expression of opinions.*

Unit 7 Gumdrop has a Birthday

Do you remember?
literal responses

Pupils should select and copy the correct sentence:
1. Whose birthday is it?   *a) It is Gumdrop's birthday.*
2. What is Gumdrop?   *b) Gumdrop is an old car.*
3. Was the birthday cake on the table?
   a) No, the cake had vanished.
4. What is the name of Mr Oldcastle's dog?
   b) The dog's name is Horace.

More to think about
sequencing

Pupils should have copied the stages for baking a cake, as follows:
Go to the shop to buy the ingredients.
Wash your hands.
Put the ingredients in a bowl.
Stir the ingredients.
Bake the mixture in the oven.
Ice the cake and put on the candles.

Now try these
deduction; character empathy

1. Write in your book 'true', 'false', 'probably' or 'can't tell' for each one of these sentences.
   a) Mr Oldcastle is very fond of Gumdrop.   *probably/true*
   b) Gumdrop is 50 years old.   *true*
   c) Mr Oldcastle is the most popular person in the village.
      can't tell
   d) The birthday cake vanished.   *true*
   e) The cake had rolled under Gumdrop.   *false*
   f) Horace had eaten the cake.   *probably*
2. Imagine you are Horace.
   Tell the story of the birthday party from your point of view.
   Notes: *Pupils might consider how the party would appear from a lower level perspective, as well as from that of a dog who can't necessarily interpret the events that are going on.*

Unit 8 An Ants' Nest

Do you remember?
cloze from passage

1. Inside an ants' nest are a mass of *tunnels* and rooms.
2. There are *three* types of ant.
3. The biggest ants are the *queens*.
4. *Worker* ants are the smallest.
5. A queen ant's main job is to lay the *eggs*.

More to think about
deductive answering in sentences; collating factual statements

1. *Pupils should write a sentence in their own words to answer each question.*
   a) What are the three types of ant?
      The three types of ant are the queens, the males and the workers.
   b) Which two types of ants have wings?
      Queen and male ants both have wings.
   c) Who looks after the young ants?
      The young ants are looked after by worker ants.
   d) Why do there need to be so many worker ants for each queen?
      The queen ants have hundreds of young and so many worker ants are needed to feed them all.
   e) Which ants have the shortest life?
      The ants with the shortest life are the males.
2. *Pupils should write a sentence in their own words to answer each question.*
   a) Write one fact about male ants.
      Male ants have wings/are bigger than worker ants/are smaller than queen ants/mate with the queen ant/die after mating.
   b) Write two facts about queen ants.
      May include: Queen ants are the biggest in the nest/ have wings/live in one room of the nest/lay hundreds of eggs.
   c) Write three facts about worker ants.
      May include: Worker ants are the smallest of the ants/ don't have wings/collect the food/feed the young ants/ keep the nest clean/dig the rooms and tunnels/defend the nest.

Now try these
lists – assessing and evaluating

1. Imagine you suddenly shrink, and become ant-sized. You explore an ants' nest. Make two lists to show in what ways ants are similar to humans, and the things that are different.
2. Ants are tiny, but when they work together they can do things they couldn't manage by themselves. Write down five things you can do alone, and five things you can do only with other people to help.

Notes: *Both assignments call for empathy with the situation, and can provide fruitful starting points for discussion and imaginative exploration prior to the commencement of written work.*

Unit 9 Thunder and Lightning

Do you remember?
selecting true sentences

Pupils should select the correct sentence from two possible choices.

1. Did this legend come from Africa?
   b) Yes, this legend came from Africa.
2. What were Thunder and Lightning?
   a) Thunder and Lightning were sheep.
3. What did Lightning do to the crops?
   a) Lightning burnt the crops.
4. Where did the village chief send them?
   a) The village chief sent them to live in the sky.

More to think about
sentence sequencing

The sentences should be ordered as follows:
3. Thunder and Lightning were two troublesome sheep.
4. The villagers became very annoyed.
6. Eventually the village chief could stand it no longer.
2. He sent them away to live in the sky.
5. Thunder still grumbles away in her loud, booming voice.
1. Lightning still upsets the villagers.
The last two sentences are interchangeable.

Now try these
vocabulary work; incident empathy

1. The following links between words with similar meanings should be made:

fed up	annoyed
complain	object to
banished	sent away
eventually	in the end
troublesome	naughty

2. Imagine that you were a villager in this legend. Write in your book about what happened, what you did about it, and how you felt.
   Notes: *In discussion, encourage pupils to consider different approaches to the problem, together with the advantages and disadvantages of each.*

Unit 10 The Lion and the Mouse

Do you remember?
assessing true/false/can't tell

Write 'true', 'false' or 'can't tell' for each of these sentences.
1. The mouse pulled the lion's tail to wake him.   *false*
2. The lion was angry.   *true*
3. He ate the little mouse.   *false*
4. When the lion was trapped the mouse released him.   *true*
5. The animals lived in Africa.   *can't tell*

More to think about
deductive answering in sentences; sequencing events

1. *Pupils should write a sentence in their own words to answer each of the questions.*
   a) What was the lion going to do when the mouse woke him?
      The lion was going to crush the mouse.
   b) What made the lion change his mind?
      The mouse pleaded that he would only be a tiny mouthful, that he would not taste good, and some day he might be able to help the lion.
   c) Who was 'the little prisoner'?
      The mouse was the little prisoner.

d) How did the mouse know the lion was in trouble?
   The mouse knew the lion was in trouble because he heard the lion's roar.
e) How did the mouse rescue the lion?
   The mouse gnawed through the ropes that bound the lion.

2. *The sentences should be ordered as follows:*
   c) A little mouse woke a lion.
   d) The lion grabbed the mouse.
   f) The lion was going to eat the mouse.
   a) The mouse persuaded the lion to set him free.
   b) The lion was trapped in the forest.
   e) The mouse helped the lion to escape.

Now try these
emotional empathy

1. Have you ever been frightened by someone bigger than you? Write some sentences about what happened and how you felt.
   Pupils will need to use empathy to 'think themselves into' this situation and explore how they felt.
2. Aesop's fables often have a moral. The moral of this story is: Don't belittle little things.
   Write what you think it means.

Notes: *Both questions may be used to help the children think about bullying.*

Progress Unit A

Do you remember?
cloze

Score: 1 mark for each correct answer (maximum 6 marks).

1. The girls were looking out of their *window*.
2. They saw a plane *crash* into the sea.
3. The pilot came down with his *parachute*.
4. The girls called for *help*.
5. A *helicopter* went to rescue the pilot.
6. The pilot gave the girls a *reward* for saving his life.

More to think about
writing sentences; interpreting pictures; classifying

Score: Q1 up to 2 marks for each sentence, depending on content and punctuation; Q2 2 marks for each complete list and 1 mark if list contains one error (maximum 18 marks).

1. Write an interesting sentence about each of the six pictures on the left.
2. Sort these into their correct lists.

Travel in the air	*helicopter plane glider hot air balloon*
Travel on land	*van bike coach car*
Travel on water	*ship ferry aircraft carrier canoe*

Now try these
character empathy

Score: award up to 2 marks for each answer, depending on the extent to which the child is empathising with the characters, as well as taking account of the content and punctuation (maximum 6 marks).

In your book write ...
1. what the telephone operator said when the girls called ...
2. what the pilot said when the helicopter arrived ...
3. what their teacher said when the girls told her the story!

Notes: *These questions call for pupils to empathise with each character.*

Indicative scores for National Curriculum

Below level 2	Level 2	Level 3
0-9	10-23	24-30

Indicative scores for 5–14 Guidelines

Level A	Level B	Level C
0-11	12-25	24-30

Unit 11 The Dragon's Cold

Do you remember?
word selection

Pupils should select the correct ending from two possible choices.

1. Mimi found a *dragon*.
2. The dragon was very *long*.
3. His name was *Duncan*.
4. He seemed rather *sad*.
5. Duncan had lost his *fire*.

More to think about
literal and deductive answering in sentences; prediction

Pupils should write a sentence in their own words to answer each question.

1. How many friends were on the beach?
   There were four friends on the beach.
2. Do you think they went to the beach to look for dragons?
   No, they didn't go to the beach to look for dragons.
3. Why were they going to run away?
   They were going to run away because they were frightened of the dragon.
4. Why had Duncan lost his fire?
   Duncan's cold had put out his fire.
5. What do you think happened in the end?
   Notes: *This question calls for pupils to think back over the story in order to predict the outcome.*

Now try these
character empathy

1. Make two lists in your book.
   List 1: The best things about being a dragon.
   List 2: The worst things about being a dragon.
2. Write about how you would have felt if you were Duncan and your family sent you away.

Notes: *These activities are intended to encourage empathy with the main character.*
Question 1 is also an early stage in assembling an argument.

Unit 12 Fun on Bikes

Do you remember?
selecting sentence endings

Pupils should copy the sentences and choose the best ending from two given possibilities in each case.

1. There is going to be a *bike-riding championship*.
2. It will be held on *Saturday 25th October*.
3. Junior events are *in the morning*.
4. Riders under 7 *are not allowed to ride*.
5. The entrance fee for adults *is £1*.

More to think about
deductive answering in sentences

Pupils should write a sentence in their own words to answer each question.

1. Where are the championships to be held?
   The championships are being held at Crossfield Farm (and/or Westergate).
2. How much does it cost to enter?
   There is no charge for riders, but adult spectators must pay £1.
3. If you are 9, what time are your races?
   Races for 9 year olds are between 10.00 and 12.30.
4. Your sister is 13. What time are her competitions?
   My sister's competition would be between 12.30 and 3.00.
5. Can you buy food and drinks after the races?
   Yes, food and drinks can be bought.

Now try these
vocabulary enrichment; emotional response

1. *The following links between words with similar meanings should be made:*

annual	once a year
championship	competition
fee	charge
spectators	audience
refreshments	things to eat and drink

2. Think carefully, then write in your book how you would feel if each of these things happened:
   a) You are given a new mountain bike as a present.
   b) The car taking you to the championships breaks down on the way.
   c) You win your first ever race.
   d) You reach the final, but then come last!
   e) Your little sister wins the cup in her event.
   Notes: *Pupils will need to use empathy to 'think themselves into' each of these situations and explore their feelings. It will be helpful, although not essential, to discuss some, if not all, of these questions before pupils write the answers. Encourage the written answers to be presented in sentences, with correct punctuation.*

Unit 13 The Owl Who Was Afraid of the Dark

Do you remember?
selecting correct answers

Match these questions and answers. *The first one has been done for pupils as an example. All the answers are given under the questions, for pupils to select from.*

1. Where was the little girl?
   The little girl was below the tree.
2. Why did Plop think the girl had a tail?
   The girl's hair was in a pony-tail.
3. Could Plop fly well?
   No, Plop couldn't fly very well.
4. What sort of owl was Plop?
   Plop was a Barn Owl.

More to think about
interpreting language; summarising

1. Which words in the story tell us that:
   a) Plop was worried about flying
      Plop shut his eyes, took a deep breath
   b) he didn't yet have his adult feathers
      woolly ball/ fluffy tummy
   c) the little girl had dirty hands?
      grubby

2. Write three sentences in your book about Plop.
   Think about his personality as well as what he looked like.
   Don't forget to use capital letters and full stops.
   Notes: *Answers may refer to Plop's age, fear of flying, bravery and determination, and his roundness and fluffy appearance.*

Now try these
vocabulary work; emotional empathy

1. The little girl said Plop was like a 'woolly ball'.
   Write in your book some words to describe these birds and animals:
   Answers may also refer to their colours:
   a) giraffe   *tall graceful slender thin agile*
   b) hippopotamus   *huge lumbering patient aggressive*
   c) robin   *delicate friendly chirpy*
   d) kitten   *inquisitive cuddly fluffy playful*
2. Have you ever been frightened of the dark, like Plop?
   Make a list of the things about the dark that can sometimes frighten people.
   Notes: *This is an opportunity for children to explore the common fear of the dark. Useful discussions can enable the children to share their feelings, but also to discover that most such fears are groundless.*

   The anxieties might be collated into a list and incorporated into a wall display.

Unit 14 Lost in the zoo

Do you remember?
cloze from passage

1. The children's names are *Dinesh* and *Indira*.
2. Their *grandparents* had taken them to the zoo.
3. They were feeding the *lambs*.
4. They didn't notice they were *lost*.
5. Luckily Indira had a *map (of the zoo)*.

More to think about
interpreting map

Pupils should write a sentence in their own words to answer each question or instruction.

1. Where were Dinesh and Indira feeding the lambs?
   They were feeding the lambs in Pets' Corner.
2. What was their quickest way back to the ticket office?
   The quickest way to the ticket office was past the pelicans, flamingos, sea lions and lions.
3. Which animals are kept closest to the ticket office?
   The lions are closest to the ticket office.
4. What type of sea animal would they have seen as they walked back to the office?
   They would have seen a sea lion.
5. Grandad left a message at the office to meet at the exit.
   Describe the best route from the office to the exit.
   Turn left at the monkey's enclosure.
6. Which creatures did they see sharing an enclosure with the pelicans?
   Flamingos were sharing an enclosure with the pelicans.
7. What animals were sharing with the zebras?
   Deer were sharing with the zebras.
8. If they had gone to the exit straight from Pets' Corner, which two roads would they have walked along?
   To reach the exit they would have walked along Bird Way and Bear Road.

Now try these
character empathy

Can you remember ever being lost? Imagine you are Dinesh or Indira and you are lost in this crowded zoo on a very hot day. Write some sentences about how you are feeling and what you are thinking.

Notes: *Pupils will need to use empathy to 'think themselves into' this situation and explore their feelings. If possible, discuss this in groups first, encouraging the children to reflect on similar situations they may have experienced.*

Unit 15 The Tale of Peter Rabbit

Do you remember?
finishing sentences

Finish these sentences.

1. Mrs Rabbit told her children they must not *go into Mr McGregor's garden.*
2. Flopsy, Mopsy and Cotton-tail went to gather *blackberries.*
3. Peter got into Mr McGregor's garden by *squeezing under the gate.*
4. When Mr McGregor saw Peter he *jumped up and ran after him.*

More to think about
question/answer matching

Match these questions and answers. *The first one has been done for pupils, as an example.*

1. What had happened to Mr Rabbit?
   Mr Rabbit had been put into a pie.
2. What did Peter eat in the garden?
   Peter ate some lettuce, French beans and radishes.
3. What was Mr McGregor doing in the garden?
   Mr McGregor was planting out young cabbages.
4. Was Peter frightened when he saw Mr McGregor?
   Peter was very frightened when he saw Mr McGregor.
5. What did Peter lose among the cabbages?
   Peter lost a shoe among the cabbages.

Now try these
vocabulary work; incident empathy

1. Copy these words from the story. Then next to each, write another word the writer could have used. The first word, 'trouble', is given for pupils, as an example.
   a) mischief   *trouble problems scrapes*
   b) among   *between in*
   c) gather   *collect pick*
   d) rushed   *ran hurried charged*
2. In your book write what Mr McGregor might have said to his wife when he went in for his tea.
   Notes: *Encourage pupils to think carefully about clues to Mr McGregor's personality, and the history of the situation.*

Unit 16 Roger the Dog

Do you remember?
selecting correct answers

Pupils should select the correct answers from two possible choices.

1. Roger only wakes to scratch his *fleas.*
2. He likes sleeping by the *fire.*
3. Roger *snores* a lot.
4. He likes eating and *sleeping* best.
5. The only hard work he does is *eating.*

More to think about
interpreting language

1. *The following links between words with similar meanings should be made (the first one has been done for pupils, as an example, 'lug him', 'carry him'):*

Poet's words	similar words
wheezes	breathes noisily
bakes	warms
lug him	carry him
romp	run and jump about
gobble and chomp	eat
flops flat	lies down

2. Find a word in the poem that rhymes with:
   a) head *bread*   b) log *dog*   c) put *foot*
   d) eyes *exercise* e) romp *chomp*   f) dish *wish*
   g) fleas *ease*   h) deep *sleep*

Now try these
character empathy; expressing reasons; simple verse writing

1. Imagine Roger is your dog. Describe what happened when you wanted to take him to the shops with you. Think about what passers by might have been saying!
   Notes: *Encourage the children to think about the character traits of their own pets, or other animals they know.*
2. If you could choose any animal as a pet, what would you choose? Write three reasons for your choice.
   Notes: *You may want to collect pupils' answers together later to consider the things which influence most children when choosing a pet.*
3. *Pupils are given an example nonsense verse, 'If I met a crocodile, I'd run a mile', and are asked to follow the same format: 'If I met a…I'd…'*
   Notes: *This can be an enjoyable class activity, which might be concluded by reading well-known nonsense verses, such as those of Edward Lear.*

Unit 17 Gran's New House

Do you remember?
cloze from passage

1. Gran and Grandad have moved to *a new house/ Sandy Bay.*
2. They moved *three* days ago.
3. From the front windows they can see the *sea.*
4. The removal truck took *six* hours to get to Sandy Bay.

More to think about
deductive answering in sentences; correcting sentence content

1. *Pupils should write a sentence in their own words to answer each question.*
   a) On which day of the week did Gran and Grandad move into their new house?
      Gran and Grandad moved on Wednesday.
   b) What will they miss most, living in Sandy Bay?
      They will miss not living in the same town as the rest of their family.
   c) What is Jenny's brother's name?
      Jenny's brother is Tim.
   d) When can the children go to visit their grandparents?
      The children can visit their grandparents in the school holidays.
   e) How might the children get to Sandy Bay if their parents are at work?
      The children would travel to Sandy Bay by train.

2. Spot the mistakes. Write the sentences correctly in your book.
   a) Gran enjoys watching the ships from the *front* window of her house/Gran enjoys watching the *hills* from the back window of her house.
   b) The hills are *at the back* of their new house/The *sea* is in front of their new house.
   c) It took *four* hours to mend the removal truck.
   d) Gran says the children *can* come and stay.
   e) Gran and Grandad will meet the children at the *station*.

Now try these
imaginative description

Describe how you imagine Gran and Grandad's new house. Write a few sentences about what it looks like and where it is.
Notes: *This is an opportunity to consider the importance of looking for as many clues as possible about settings in literature and the children's own writing. Collecting appropriate adjectives would be a useful introductory activity.*

Unit 18 Hot Dog Harris

Do you remember?
cloze from passage

1. Hot Dog was a Yorkshire *terrier*.
2. He lived with the *Harris* family.
3. They all lived in a town called *Barnsley*.
4. The children were called *Harold* and *Hattie*.
5. Grandad said Hot Dog looked like a *wig* on legs.

More to think about
correcting sentence content; deductive answering in sentences

1. One word in each sentence doesn't make sense. Write each sentence correctly.
   a) Harold's *sister* was called Hattie.
   b) Hot Dog was the *smallest* dog in the world.
   c) Their grandad *teased (or similar)* the little creature.
2. Pupils should write a sentence in their own words to answer each question.
   a) Why do you think the dog was called 'Hot Dog'?
   The little dog was called Hot Dog because he was about the size of a hot dog sausage.
   b) Why did old Mr Harris call him 'a wig on legs'?
   Old Mr Harris thought the dog's long, shaggy hair made him look like a wig.
   c) Why did the family want to keep Hot Dog in the house?
   Notes: *This question requires pupils to draw inferences from the text, for example, he might get lost/stolen/run-over.*

Now try these
character empathy; imaginative description

1. Pretend you are Hot Dog. Copy the description boxes neatly into your book. Write two ideas in each box.
   Notes: *This activity is intended to help pupils to structure their thinking when there is more than one variable in an argument. Pupils are given a table in which they should write: 'Good things about being small' (this answer has been given as an example), 'Good things about being big', 'Bad things about being small', 'Bad things about being big'.*
2. One day Hot Dog managed to escape from the house. Describe one of the adventures he might have had.
   Notes: *Encourage preliminary consideration of Hot Dog's physical features/character to determine the types of problems he might encounter.*

Unit 19 Funny Feeders

Do you remember?
cloze from passage

1. Some toads have long *tongues*.
2. Vultures wait for animals to *die* (or *be killed*).
3. Venus fly traps catch *insects* in their leaves.
4. Mistletoe grows in *(the branches of) trees*.
5. Mosquitoes and fleas are both called *parasites*.

More to think about
deductive answering in sentences

Pupils should write a sentence in their own words to answer each question.
1. Why are vultures good for the environment?
   They clear away dead creatures which could spread diseases.
2. Why would it be bad for the parasite if it killed the plant or animal it lives on?
   If a parasite kills its 'host' it destroys its home and supply of food.
3. Why is mistletoe becoming a rare plant in many places?
   Answers may include: over-harvesting for Christmas; fewer birds to transport seeds; fewer trees (especially following Dutch Elm Disease).
4. If you squash a mosquito it leaves a red mark. Why?
   The red is blood from previous feeds.

Now try these
character empathy; imaginative description

Imagine you are a creature that has just arrived from outer space. You have never seen humans before. Write a report about how these strange human creatures feed. Start like this, or make up your own beginning if you prefer:
First they dig up funny lumpy things from the ground, which they put into boiling water. They also put other plants in hot water and watch them go all squidgy and squashy.
Notes: *This activity is devised to encourage detailed, close analysis of a common function of human behaviour. Other functions, such as walking, sleeping, or games, could have the same activity applied to them.*

Unit 20 Big Bulgy Black Fat Slugs

Do you remember?
cloze

1. The poet doesn't like *slugs*.
2. She says they are wobbly and wet in the long *grass*.
3. They leave their slippery trails along the *path*.
4. She doesn't want them to get between her *toes*.
5. She definitely wouldn't want a slug as a *pet*.

More to think about
making sense of sentences

Look at the poem again. One word in each sentence doesn't make sense. Write each sentence correctly.
1. Slugs are usually *black*.
2. They *creep* through wet grass.
3. When they *slide* they leave a slippery trail.
4. Slugs *squidge* between your toes.

Now try these
vocabulary work; incident empathy

1. Write the words the poet uses to describe these.
   The first one has been done for pupils, as an example.
   a) what slugs look like   *big bulgy black*

b) how slugs look when they creep *soft and slimy and squashy, wobbly and wet*

c) how slugs look when they slide *squelchy*

d) how slugs feel if you touch them *cold and slithery*

2. Make a list of your four favourite creatures. Say why you like each one.

   Notes: *This asks for an empathetic response from the children.*

3. Make a list of four creatures you don't like. Say what it is you don't like about each one.

   Notes: *In discussion distinguish between objective and subjective opinions.*

4. Imagine the slug could understand English, and heard people saying unkind and rude things about him. How would he feel, and what might he say back?

   Notes: *This activity seeks to establish empathy with the slug. A useful follow-up is for the children to 'perform' their works as simple monologues.*

Progress Unit B

Do you remember?
cloze

Score: 1 mark for each correct answer (maximum 8 marks).

May-May and *Rose*, the two Golly sisters, couldn't make their *horse* go. The *wagon* was loaded, and they had practised their *songs* and *dances*. The sisters got very *mad*, but the horse still wouldn't go! Then Rose remembered you need to say *Giddy-up* to tell a horse to go.

More to think about
deductive answering in sentences; summarising; outcome prediction

Score: Q1 2 marks for each correct answer; Q2 2 marks for each of the three components; Q3 3 marks for a plausible answer (maximum 19 marks).

1. Pupils should write a sentence in their own words to answer each question.

   a) Where were the Golly sisters going?
      They were going west (across America).

   b) How do you know they didn't drive wagons very often?
      The sisters didn't know how to tell a horse to move forward.

   c) Was the horse well trained or badly trained?
      The horse was well trained.

   d) Were they right to get cross with the horse?
      No, they were not right to get cross with the horse.

   e) Did getting cross with the horse make it go?
      No, the horse didn't move when they got cross with it.

2. Write a short version of the story so far, using no more than three sentences.

   Notes: *This question tests pupils' summary skills. The three most significant events for pupils to spot are: the sisters intending to go west (to earn their living as performers); their ignorance about driving a horse and wagon; the discovery that with the correct instruction the horse would move.*

3. How do you think the story of the Golly sisters might have ended?

   Notes: *Pupils may predict either short-term outcomes, such as losing the horse as it gallops off with their belongings, or longer-term outcomes, such as a successful or disastrous adventure.*

Now try these
incident empathy

Score: up to 5 marks for a clear and cogent account of a 'frustrating' situation (maximum 3 marks).

Think of a time when something didn't happen that you have really wanted to happen, like:

when you couldn't make a new computer game work,
or when you couldn't get the chain back on your bike,
or when someone you had been expecting didn't turn up.

Notes: *This activity tests the child's ability to transfer knowledge from a personal experience and empathise with the type of incident portrayed in the passage.*

Indicative scores for National Curriculum

Below level 2	Level 2	Level 3
0-9	10-23	24-30

Indicative scores for 5–14 Guidelines

Level A	Level B	Level C
0-11	12-25	26-30

FOCUS

on Comprehension

Book 2

Scope and sequence of skills

Unit	Title	Page	Do you remember? *Reading the lines*	More to think about *Reading between the lines*	Now try these *Reading beyond the lines*
1	**The Eagle and the Turtle** *Aesop's Fable*	4	cloze from passage	deductive answering in sentences; summarising	empathy with situations and characters; interpreting 'morals'
2	**On the Move** *Factual text and diagram*	6	word selection	ordering by size; deductive responses	environmental considerations of transportation modes
3	**Growing** *Life cycles in pictorial and poetic form*	8	relating text to picture	sequencing	empathy with the Frog Prince
4	**Three Girls** *Modern fiction*	10	selecting correct answer	deductive answering in sentences; summarising	character empathy; rhyme
5	**On Holiday** *Leaflet/rules and map*	12	cloze from passage	deductive answering in sentences; figurative language	evaluating statements
6	**Magic** *Modern poem*	14	matching questions/ answers	true/false/can't tell deductive responses	situation empathy
7	**What's It All About?** Book cover and contents page	16	cloze	deductive answering with words or numbers	application of skills
8	**Tim the Trumpet** *Modern fiction*	18	extended cloze from passage	literal answering in sentences	appreciation of similes

Book 2

Unit	Title	Page	Do you remember? _Reading the lines_	More to think about _Reading between the lines_	Now try these _Reading beyond the lines_
9	**The Wind in the Willows** _Long-established fiction_	20	selecting true sentences	deductive answering in sentences; working with phrases	vocabulary work; incident empathy
10	**I Love Our Orange Tent** _Modern poem_	22	cloze	deductive answering in sentences	incident empathy using list making
	Progress Unit A _Newspaper article_	24	true/false/can't tell literal responses	writing questions	incident empathy; vocabulary activity
11	**The Swoose** _Modern fiction_	26	selecting correct answer	deductive answering in sentences; nonsense word building	vocabulary work; character empathy; story completion
12	**The Dragon's Egg** _Traditional story_	28	cloze from words listed	sequencing sentences; deductive answering in sentences	vocabulary work; character empathy
13	**What is...the Sun?** _Modern poem and information text_	30	selecting correct answers	using grid; interpreting metaphors; evaluating	further metaphor activity
14	**Dr Xargle and the Earthlets** _Map_	32	selecting correct words	deductive answering in sentences	using descriptive language
15	**Feathered Record Breakers** _Reference text_	34	selecting correct answers	true/false/can't tell deductive responses	incident empathy; vocabulary work
16	**Bus Route** _Modern poem_	36	selecting correct words	deductive answering in sentences; interpreting language	character empathy
17	**A Day When Frogs Wear Shoes** _Modern text from the Caribbean_	38	extended cloze from passage	deductive answering in sentences	character description; situation empathy
18	**Basilisks** _Myth_	40	cloze from passage; literal answers in sentences	interpretation of figurative language	character empathy; retelling myth of choice
19	**Mrs Wobble the Waitress** _Modern fiction_	42	selecting true sentences	working with phrases; outcome prediction; summarising	critical evaluation of content
20	**Humans – friends or foes?** _Nigerian poem Indian art_	44	selecting correct answers	deductive answering in sentences	arguing a case
	Progress Unit B _Modern fiction Child's poem_	46	sentence completion; literal answers in sentences	interpretation of figurative language	character empathy

Unit 1 The Eagle and the Turtle

Do you remember?
cloze from passage

1. The Turtle wanted to be able to _fly_ in the sky.
2. He went to speak to the _Eagle_ about it.
3. The Eagle said he couldn't fly because he didn't have _wings_.
4. The Turtle promised the Eagle rare _pearls_ if he helped him.
5. When he tried to fly he fell like a _stone_.

More to think about
deductive answering in sentences; summarising

1. Pupils should write a sentence in their own words to answer each question.
   a) What words does the Turtle use to describe how he would like to fly?
      The Turtle said that he wanted to be able to fly in the air like an eagle.
   b) What does he have that he thinks will help him to fly?
      He thinks that his flippers will help him to fly.

40

c) How can we tell that the Eagle doesn't want to carry the Turtle high in the sky?
The Eagle told the Turtle that he was not built for flying.
d) How does the Turtle persuade the Eagle to help him?
He promises to give the Eagle pearls if he helps him to fly.
e) How does the writer describe how the Turtle fell?
The Turtle fell like a stone.
2. Write the story in your own words in a short form. Try to use no more than three sentences.
Notes: *The ability to precis longer pieces of writing is a useful skill, but also a good indicator of whether the reader*
has thoroughly understood the passage. However, it is a skill that needs teaching, which can usefully be done as a regular activity with the class as a whole or in groups.

Now try these
empathy with situations and characters; interpreting 'morals'

1. *Pupils should write an ending to each sentence in their own words.*
a) The Turtle was not satisfied with his life because *he was tired of swimming about in the sea and crawling about on the beach, getting nowhere in particular.*
b) He thought that if only he could fly he would be able to *see new things and visit new places.*
c) The Eagle really didn't want to carry the Turtle into the sky because *he knew that it would be impossible for the Turtle to fly, and so he would be killed.*
2. a) Write two good things and two bad things about being a turtle.
b) Write two good things and two bad things about being an eagle.
Notes: *These activities, usefully introduced through group discussion, enable the children to blend knowledge from other sources with that gained from reading the passage.*
3. There are two morals to this fable:
Be satisfied with what you are.
The higher you fly, the harder you may fall.
Write in your own words what each means.
Notes: *This work may be extended by collecting and discussing other morals.*

Unit 2 On the Move

Do you remember?
word selection

Pupils should select the correct answer from two possible choices.
1. An oil tanker carries *oil.*
2. Aeroplanes are *faster* than ships.
3. Trucks can carry *less* than trains.
4. Buses and coaches carry *people.*
5. Most people prefer to travel by *car.*

More to think about
ordering by size; deductive responses

1. List the things in this picture:
a) that carry freight.
oil tanker, train, lorry
b) that carry people.
aeroplane, train, bus, car
2. What would be the best way to:
a) move food from a factory to the shops? *trucks (or lorries) and vans*
b) get your class to the local swimming pool? *coach or bus*

c) bring oil from 2000 kilometres away? *sea oil tanker*
d) get to Spain on holiday? *aeroplane*
e) move large amounts of coal to a power station? *railway/freight train*

Now try these
environmental considerations of transportation modes
Notes: *The development of the ability to debate and discuss, distinguishing fact and opinion, is important. As appropriate, some children may be encouraged to supplement the information contained in this unit by further research, including opinion surveying, before completing the activities.*
1. Write sentences to answer these questions.
a) Why do people usually like to travel by car if they have one?
Answers may revolve around convenience – they can get door-to-door; they can often travel faster and with less 'hassle' than on public transport; they can be used more flexibly; they are cheaper for families.
b) What problems can there be about travelling by car?
Answers will include: congestion; boredom; finding your way.
c) Why is it better if more goods can be sent by train?
Answers will include: less congestion on roads; reduced pollution.
d) Do you think more people should travel by bike? Give your reasons.
This question also encourages environmental considerations.
2. Write a letter to your Member of Parliament giving all the reasons why a new airport should not be built in fields near to your house.

Unit 3 Growing

Do you remember?
relating text to picture
Read the poem and look carefully at the pictures.
Copy the lines from the poem
1. ...that most closely match picture number 1.
Tadpoles are fat round dots.
2. ...that most closely match picture number 2.
They stand on their toes to nibble weed.
3. ...that most closely match picture number 4.
A head with a tail.

More to think about
sequencing
1. *Pupils are told that the sentences from an information book have been muddled up. The sentences should be sequenced in this order:*
The frog lays her eggs, called frog spawn.
Little tadpoles grow inside the jelly.
The tadpoles hatch from the jelly.
Soon their rear legs begin to grow.
Their tails get shorter, and disappear.
The tadpoles have become frogs.
2. Imagine that you are writing an information book. Write some sentences to describe the order of what happens from the time when you buy some bulbs until you have some beautiful flowers.
Notes: *Pupils will answer based on the illustrations provided. Sequencing of information is an important studying and comprehension skill, and can be developed and practised with work based on literature passages as well as non-fiction. Some pupils will find it helpful to base*

the work, at least initially, on concrete examples, such as the events occurring from getting up in the morning to arriving at school.

Now try these
empathy with the Frog Prince

1. In the fairy story the prince was turned into a frog. Pretend you were the prince. Write about how it felt not being able to tell anyone that you were not really a frog, but a person.
2. Tell the story of some scary or funny things that happened to you.

Notes: *These two questions, in encouraging pupils to empathise with the frog, may lead to some interesting consideration of our basic anxieties about being imprisoned and restrained. For some children, it will have pertinent echoes if a relative has been imprisoned, and so needs careful handling.*

Unit 4 Three Girls

Do you remember?
selecting correct answer

Pupils should select and copy out the correct answer from a choice of two possible answers.

1. Are there three girls walking along the beach?
   b) Yes, there are three girls walking along the beach.
2. What did the girls come to?
   a) They came to a cave.
3. What is inside the cave?
   b) There is gold in the cave.
4. Why do the first and second girls run out of the cave?
   b) They are frightened by a ghost.
5. Is the third girl brave enough to enter the cave?
   a) Yes, the third girl goes into the cave.

More to think about
deductive answering in sentences; summarising

1. *Pupils should write a sentence in their own words to answer each question.*
   a) Did the first girl plan to share the gold with her friends?
   The first girl thought she would keep all the gold for herself.
   b) How might the gold have come to be in the cave?
   The gold was probably deposited in the cave following a shipwreck.
   c) Why might the ghost of Captain Cox think the gold was his?
   He was probably the captain of the ship which had been carrying the gold.
   d) Was the ghost successful in protecting the gold?
   No, because the third girl was not frightened of the ghost.
2. Write the story in your own words. Don't use more than 40 words.

Now try these
character empathy; rhyme

1. Make a list of all the dangers there could be in a cave.
   Answers may include: becoming trapped by the tide; falling rocks; hidden pot-holes; broken glass and other debris.
2. Write in your book how you would have felt if:
   a) you had been the first girl b) you had been the third girl
   Notes: *Class or group discussion before the activity is undertaken will encourage pupils to compare and contrast the two characters.*

3. In your book, write what is being said.
   Notes: *This is a useful opportunity to introduce, or revisit, the difference between 'direct' and 'indirect', or reported, speech. It might also be extended for some children into writing a small play based on the passage.*
4. Find a word in the poem to rhyme with
   a) Cox *rocks* b) Crocket *pocket*
   Notes: *You can extend this by finding other rhyming words, and categorising them into groups with common spelling patterns.*

Unit 5 On Holiday

Do you remember?
cloze from passage

1. Our family went to *Sandy Bay Holiday Park* for our holiday.
2. When we arrived we were given instructions and a *map*.
3. The instructions suggested the first thing to do was *walk* around the park.
4. When we went to the bar they gave us a free *drink*.
5. Nobody was allowed in the swimming pool after *9 p.m.*

More to think about
deductive answering in sentences; figurative language

1. *Pupils should write a sentence in their own words to answer each question.*
   a) How far is it to the beach?
   It's about half a mile (one kilometre) to the beach.
   b) What is the nearest town?
   The nearest town is Moreton.
   c) Is the Motor Sports theme park close enough to walk to?
   No, the theme park is probably too far to walk (2 miles).
   d) Where is the zoo?
   It's in Scarmouth.
   e) What might be the best thing for the family to do when it rains?
   The family could go to the indoor amusement park when it rains.
2. What do each of these phrases mean?
   a) help you find your feet
   help you settle in quickly
   b) to stock up with provisions
   to buy food and other essential requirements
   c) with the compliments of the management
   free, to say thank you for coming
   d) away from the hurly-burly of everyday life
   away from work and problems of normal living
   e) unaccompanied children
   children who are not with an adult

Now try these
evaluating statements

Notes: *These activities require consideration of the reasons for, and desirability and acceptability of, certain situations. Such work is often enhanced if preceded by oral work in a group or class lesson context.*

1. What reasons could the management have for suggesting that one of the first things to do is to go to the supermarket?
   to make a sale before clients find shops (possibly less expensive) off-site; to ensure new-comers have essentials before shop closes
2. Why would they ask that everyone has returned to the park by 11.30 p.m.?
   to settle the camp down at a reasonable time for those

who want to sleep undisturbed; for reasons of security; to control noisier holiday-makers

3. Do you agree that children under 7 should not be allowed to swim without an adult?
   Notes: *This question calls for pupils to consider the reasons for the rule and make a judgement.*

4. If you were the manager of the holiday park, what rules would you make?
   Notes: *This builds on the previous question and requires pupils to have considered and understood what the rules are for. Pupils are asked to write the rules out neatly so as to encourage them to think about their audience.*

Unit 6 Magic

Do you remember?
matching questions/answers

Match these questions and answers.
The first one has been done for pupils, as an example.

What did Sandra see?	*She saw a leprechaun.*
Who danced with the witches?	*Laurie danced with them.*
What did Charlie find?	*He found some goblin's gold.*
Who was singing?	*A mermaid was singing.*
What did Eddie touch?	*He touched a troll.*

More to think about
true/false/can't tell deductive responses

From what it says in the poem, write in your book 'true', 'false', or 'can't tell' for each of these sentences.

1. Sandra likes leprechauns. *can't tell*
2. Eddie has seen a troll. *true*
3. Witches can dance. *true*
4. Laurie often dances with witches. *false*
5. The goblin's gold was hidden in a cave. *can't tell*
6. Mermaids only sing sea-shanties. *can't tell*
7. Susie talked to an elf. *can't tell*
8. The elf was in Susie's garden. *can't tell*

Now try these
situation empathy

Notes: *You may decide to use the first of these activities with the whole class, and follow this by allowing pupils to select one of the other two to be written individually. Support and encouragement for many pupils will be needed if the children are to empathise fully, rather than give shallow, short answers.*

1. In your book write:
   a) something your teacher might say when she finds a goblin under her table
   b) something your mum might say when you bring a witch home to tea
   c) something your friend might say when you explain about a family of elves that you have seen under a bush on your way to school.

2. What does the poet mean when he says:
   'But all the magic I have known
   I've had to make myself?'
   The poet believes that the various people mentioned have actually witnessed the events described, whereas he recognises that he can only achieve such fantasies in his imagination.

Unit 7 What's It All About?

Do you remember?
cloze

1. The book is in a series called *Science* World.
2. The title of the book is *Light*.
3. It is written by *Mark Morris*.
4. The first chapter is called *Daylight*.
5. The last chapter is about *Playing with shadows*.

More to think about
deductive answering with words or numbers

Answer these quick questions with a word or a number.
1. What is chapter 3 about? *reflections*
2. In which chapter can I read about rainbows? *chapter 5*
3. How many chapters are there in the book? *6*
4. On which page can I begin to read about eyes? *page 18*
5. How many pages are there in chapter 5? *2*
6. How many pages are there in chapter 2? *6*
7. In which chapter might I find out about the moon? *chapter 2*
8. In which chapter might I find out about mirrors? *chapter 3*
9. Write the title of another book that you might expect to find in this series. *A science topic should be specified.*
10. What is the name of the publisher of the book? *Collins Educational*

Now try these
application of skills

Notes: *These non-fiction research skills are important and so, while this activity relates to two titles, it is an exercise to which you may choose to return from time to time. The work can be extended by presenting a group with several information books on a theme, and inviting the group to compare and contrast them, and consider their ease of use.*
Find in your library *two* books which interest you.
Answer these questions for each one:
1. What is the title of the book?
2. Who is the author?
3. What is the name of the publisher?
4. What is the book about?
5. How many chapters are in the book?
6. How many pages are in the book?
7. On which page does the first chapter begin?
8. On which page does chapter 3 begin?
9. What is the title of the second chapter?
10. What do you most like about the book?

Unit 8 Tim the Trumpet

Do you remember?
extended cloze from passage

Pupils should note that the following words are missing:
1. *Tim* 2. *clean* 3. *T-shirt* 4. *voice* 5. *baby*
6. *neighbours* 7. *police* 8. *Vicar*

More to think about
literal answering in sentences

Pupils should write sentences in their own words to answer each question.
1. In the story Tim's voice is described as being like other loud noises.
   a) What was it like when he was a baby?
      Tim's voice when he was a baby was like an alarm bell going off.

b) What noises was it like when he got older?

Later it became like a cross between a factory hooter and a foghorn, or a roll of thunder and a ship's siren.

2. Describe what Tim usually looked like.

Tim was normally rather scruffy, with untidy hair and a grubby face, and with his clothes dusty and disorganised.

3. Why did the neighbours think they should call the police?

They thought something terrible was happening to Tim.

4. Did Tim make loud noises because his parents were unkind to him?

No, Tim couldn't help making loud noises every time he spoke.

5. How did the Vicar know he should wear ear muffs?

The Vicar had been warned about Tim's very loud voice.

Now try these
appreciation of similes

1. Copy these sentences, and neatly underline the similes.

An explanation of similes has been given for pupils. The first one has also been done for them, as an example.

a) Tim's voice was <u>like a foghorn</u>.

b) Tim's mother thought her baby was <u>as pretty as a picture</u>.

c) Some people said Tim's voice was <u>like a ship's siren</u>.

d) When Tim was a baby he sounded <u>as loud as an alarm bell</u>.

e) When Tim was older he could call across the playground <u>as easy as pie</u>.

Notes: *This activity can be extended: discuss what each simile means by considering its context.*

2. Which creature do you think of to finish these similes?

Pupils are given names in a box, to help them.

a) as brave as a *lion*   f) as happy as a *lark*

b) as cunning as a *fox*   g) as slow as a *tortoise*

c) as timid as a *rabbit*   h) as obstinate as a *mule*

d) as quiet as a *mouse*   i) as slippery as an *eel*

e) as fast as a *hare*   j) as wise as an *owl*

Notes: *Make a class collection of similes that are currently in use, and also make up similes – a useful exercise in vocabulary enrichment as well as being supportive of reading comprehension.*

Unit 9 The Wind in the Willows

Do you remember?
selecting true sentences

Read these sentences about the story. Copy only the ones that are true.

1. Mole lived by the river.

3. He could see the Water Rat on the opposite bank.

5. The Rat had a boat.

6. The boat was painted blue and white.

More to think about
deductive answering in sentences; working with phrases

1. *Pupils should write a sentence in their own words to answer each question.*

a) How did Mole know the twinkle he saw on the opposite bank was not a star?

Mole knew a star would not be in that position.

b) Was Rat's boat large or small?

Rat's boat was small.

c) What words tell us that Mole was excited when he first saw the boat?

Mole's whole heart went out to it.

d) Why was Mole rather unsure about getting into Rat's boat?

Mole had never been in a boat before.

2. *Pupils are given groups of words under three columns, headed: 'Who?', 'Did what?', 'Where?'. They are asked to take a group of words out of each column to make a sensible sentence. Their sentences should be:*

The Mole sat on the grass.

The Rat came out of his hole.

The Rat sculled across the river.

Now try these
vocabulary work; incident empathy

1. What words does the author use:

a) to describe Rat's face?

a brown little face, with whiskers; a grave round face, with a twinkle in its eye; (some pupils may also add – small neat ears and thick silky hair)

b) to describe how Rat brought the boat across the river?

Rat sculled smartly across.

c) to describe how Mole got into the boat?

Mole stepped gingerly down.

2. Think back to when you did something for the first time, and describe your feelings. Were you frightened or excited, or a bit of both? What other feelings did you have?

Notes: *This is an opportunity to explore emotional reactions to a story. These will often be derived from related first-hand experiences. It is a useful group discussion topic, to be covered before individuals write their own answers to the question.*

Unit 10 I Love Our Orange Tent

Do you remember?
cloze

1. The children love their orange *tent*.

2. They put it up in the *garden*.

3. At night they can hear the *owl* crying.

4. When the wind blows, the tent *flaps*.

5. They like being in the tent best when the sun is *shining*.

More to think about
deductive answering in sentences

Pupils should write a sentence in their own words to answer each question.

1. Why does the poet say that they plant the tent like a flower in the field?

The tent is a bright colour and looks like a flower on the green lawn, that looks like a small field.

2. Does she like the smell of the grass in the orange tent?

Yes, she says it smells sweet.

3. What does the tent sound like when the wind blows?

When the wind blows it sounds like a bird flapping its wings.

4. Do you think the fourth verse describes heavy rain or light rain? Give your reasons.

The fourth verse describes fairly light rain, because it describes it as having the sound of tiny footsteps.

5. Why does the poet like being in the tent most when the sun shines?

When the sun is shining the tent glows a bright gold colour, reminding the poet of yellow honey.

Now try these
incident empathy using list making

Imagine that the orange tent is your tent.
1. What do you think are the best things about going camping?
   Make a list.
2. Now make a list of all the problems that could happen on a camping trip.
   Notes: *This activity is most effective if, after a brief discussion, the pupils work in pairs or alone to 'think themselves into' the situation of going camping. You can then bring everyone together for a discussion afterwards.*

Progress Unit A

Do you remember?
true/false/can't tell literal responses

Score: 1 mark for each correct answer (maximum 5 marks).

Write in your book 'true', 'false', or 'can't tell' for each one.
1. Mrs Wills had been walking with her husband.   *false*
2. She was wearing a red coat and blue scarf.   *can't tell*
3. It was very unusual for the River Thames to freeze right across.   *true*
4. There was nobody around to help Mrs Wills.   *false*
5. The dog managed to scramble to safety.   *can't tell*

More to think about
writing questions

Score: Q1 1 mark for each correct answer (maximum 4 marks); Q2 1 mark for each of 9 main points plus 1 for keeping within about 60 words (maximum 14 marks).

1. *Pupils are given answers to five questions about the newspaper article and they are asked to provide the questions. The first one has been done for pupils as an example.*
   a) Mrs Wills was 79.
      How old was Mrs Wills? (no mark – answer provided)
   b) She went onto the ice to rescue the dog.
      Why did she go onto the ice?
   c) It was a black labrador dog.
      What was the colour and breed of dog that Mrs Wills was walking?
   d) The Rescue Services arrived within five minutes.
      How long did it take for the Rescue Services to reach the scene?
   e) Last week they tried to save an eight year old boy.
      Who had they been called out to rescue last week?
2. The newspaper editor has said the article is too long. Re-write the article in your own words in no more than 60 words.
   Notes: *Ensure all the salient points are mentioned: Mrs Wills walking dog; frozen river; dog chases duck; dog gets stuck; rescue attempt; Mrs Wills falls through ice; Rescue Services not able to save her; second accident in a week.*

   Consider keeping other interesting articles from local and national press which children can use to practise precis work.

Now try these
incident empathy; vocabulary activity

Score: Q1 award up to 2 marks for each list if consideration is given to other people/creatures, 1 mark if list relates only to self; Q2 award up to 3 marks for clear account which accords with detail given in the article; Q3 1 mark for each correct usage (maximum 11 marks).

1. Make two lists, one with the good things about winter and another with the bad things about winter. Try to think of other people and creatures, as well as yourself.
2. Imagine that you were walking along the bank of the river just as the dog went onto the ice. You could see the possible danger ahead for the old lady. Write about what you would have done, without putting yourself in danger.
   Notes: *The first two questions require pupils to use empathy to 'think themselves into' the particular situations and think about feelings/what to do.*
3. Write sentences of your own to show that you know what each of these words mean:
   a) fatality   b) tragedy   c) elderly   d) desperately

Indicative scores for National Curriculum

Below level 2	Level 2	Level 3	Level 4
0-4	5-14	15-26	27-30

Indicative scores for 5–14 Guidelines

Level A	Level B	Level C
0-5	6-18	19-30

Unit 11 The Swoose

Do you remember?
selecting correct answer

Pupils should choose the correct ending from three possible choices.
1. Fitzherbert's mother was   *c) a goose*
2. Fitzherbert thought he was   *a) a goose*
3. He had always thought his father was
   a) the old grey gander
4. His mother told him about his father
   a) in a corner of the farmyard
5. His mother told Fitzherbert that his father was
   c) a white swan

More to think about
deductive answering in sentences; nonsense word building

1. *Pupils should write a sentence in their own words to answer each question.*
   a) What clue does the author give us near the beginning that Fitzherbert might be related to a swan?
      Fitzherbert was able to coil his neck back into the shape of an S.
   b) Why did his mother want to tell him away from the other geese?
      She didn't want the other geese to know that she had had an affair with a swan.
   c) What words does the author use to show that Fitzherbert's mother was very fond of his real father?
      The author says that a dreamy look came over her face as she spoke about the white swan.

2. If a swoose has a swan father and a goose mother, write the name for a creature which is a cross between:
a) a shark and a whale   *shale/whark*
b) a bat and a robin   *bobin*
c) a pig and a cow   *pow/cig*
Choose one and describe its looks and unusual ways.
Notes: *As an additional activity, the children might illustrate their fictitious animal characters and/or use them in various types of writing tasks.*

Now try these
vocabulary work; character empathy; story completion

1. What do the following phrases mean?
a) lowered her voice   *spoke more quietly*
b) out of earshot   *far enough away to not be heard*
c) white as the driven snow   *pure white*
2. If you were the swoose, describe how you would feel when your mother gave you the surprise news about your father.
This calls for pupils to empathise with the swoose.
3. This is the beginning of a story. Write a few sentences to tell how, if you were the author, you would finish the story of the swoose.
Notes: *Encourage children to share and discuss their varying responses, and to discuss the likely validity of each, taking account of any clues that exist to character traits which can be detected in the passage.*

Unit 12 The Dragon's Egg

Do you remember?
cloze from words listed

1. A *man* and a *dragon* were friends.
2. The dragon collected *silver* and *gold*.
3. He had to go away on a long *journey*.
4. The dragon didn't *trust* the man.
5. The man tried to steal the dragon's *treasure*.

More to think about
sequencing sentences; deductive answering in sentences

1. The sentences should be sequenced in the following order:
The dragon had a lot of treasure.
He asked the man to look after his gold and silver.
The man tried to kill the dragon and keep the treasure.
The dragon came back and was very upset.
He ate the man for supper.
2. Pupils should write a sentence in their own words to answer each question.
a) Why at first did the dragon think he could trust the man?
The dragon thought he could trust the man as he was a close friend.
b) Why did he change his mind about trusting the man?
He was worried that the man's greed for the gold might make him untrustworthy.
c) Did the man always intend to steal the treasure?
No, but the temptation grew stronger until he could no longer resist.
d) Why didn't the dragon die when the man broke the egg?
The dragon had misled the man into thinking he would die if the egg was broken.

Now try these
vocabulary enrichment; empathy

1. Find words in the passage that mean:
a) collected   *gathered together*
b) very big   *huge*
c) wish or want   *desire*
d) a small box   *casket*
2. In your book write ...
a) something your teacher might say if a dragon came up to the classroom window
b) three things you might do if you suddenly became very rich.
Notes: *These questions call for pupils to show empathy for their teacher and also to use empathy to 'think themselves into' a particular situation in order to explore their feelings.*

Unit 13 What is...the Sun?

Do you remember?
selecting correct answers

Pupils are asked to choose the right ending from three possible endings.
1. Most stars are *bigger than the Sun.*
2. The Sun is made of *fiery gases.*
3. From Earth to the Sun is *nearly 150 million kilometres.*
4. Once every year *the Earth travels around the Sun.*

More to think about
using grid; interpreting metaphors; evaluating

1. Use the grid to answer the questions.
The first one has been done for pupils as an example.
a) How many planets, apart from Earth, does the Sun have?   *C1*
b) How many times bigger than the Sun are some other stars?   *C3*
c) What two important things does the Sun give to Earth?   *A2 and B1*
d) How many days does the Earth take to circle the Sun?   *B2*
e) How many years does the Earth take to circle the Sun?   *A3*
f) Which is the nearest star to Earth?   *C2*
g) What is the Sun made of?   *B3*
2. The poet cleverly compares the Sun with other things.
a) What is 'the calm sea' in the first verse?   *the sky*
b) Where does the poet think heaven is, in the second verse?   *above the sky*
c) What is the 'sheet of pale blue paper', in the fourth verse?   *the blue sky*
d) Which verse do you like best? Why?
Notes: *This question calls for pupils to evaluate the poem in order to give reasons for their choice.*

Now try these
further metaphor activity

Poets often compare things. It helps them to write strong, vivid poems. Write down three things which remind you of each of these.
1. The sea
2. A snake
3. An ants' nest
Notes: *This question calls for pupils to create metaphors. Encourage pupils to explore a range of poetry books to find, and perhaps make a collection of, other poems with strong metaphors. Poetry readings of such poems can form a good conclusion to a class lesson.*

Unit 14 Dr Xargle and the Earthlets

Do you remember?
selecting correct words

Pupils should select the correct words from two possible choices.

1. The teacher is giving a lesson about *Earthlets*.
2. Earthlets are never *green*.
3. They grow fur on their *heads*.
4. They are patted to stop them *crying*.
5. If they still cry they are sent to *beddybyes*.

More to think about
deductive answering in sentences

1. Pupils should write a sentence in their own words to answer each question.
   a) What is an Earthlet?
      An Earthlet is a human.
   b) On which planet do they live?
      They live on Earth.
   c) What are the 'two short tentacles with pheelers on the end'?
      The tentacles are arms.
   d) Who or what are Tibbles and Marmaduke?
      Tibbles and Marmaduke are cats.
   e) What do we call 'eggmangle on a small spade'?
      Eggmangle on a small spade is scrambled egg on a spoon.
2. Use the clues in the passage to answer these questions about the unknown planet billions and trillions of miles away.
   a) What colour are the people who live there?
      green (they note this as the only colour)
   b) Do they have more than or fewer than two eyes?
      more than two eyes (humans have '...only two')
   c) What keeps these strange people warm?
      fur (they are surprised humans only have fur on their heads)
   d) Would you expect them to have large teeth?
      yes (they refer to 'fangs')
   e) Would you expect to find other creatures on their planet?
      yes (they know about 'wild beasts')

Now try these
using descriptive language

Imagine that your spacecraft has just secretly visited Planet Earth from this unknown planet. Choose one of these things you have been watching, and write in your book how you will explain it to people when you return to your own planet.
a) a cricket match   b) a train   c) a beach   d) a classroom
Notes: *This is an activity that most children enjoy, and which enables them to practise their analytical skills. Encourage the children to clear their minds as much as possible of preconceived ideas, and to thoroughly analyse the situations and events.*

Unit 15 Feathered Record Breakers

Do you remember?
selecting correct answers

Pupils should write a sentence in their own words to answer each question.

1. Where are ostriches found in the wild?
   Ostriches live in the wild in Africa.
2. How fast can the spine-tailed swift fly?
   The spine-tailed swift can fly at 170 kilometres per hour.

3. Which bird has the widest wingspan?
   Albatrosses have the widest wingspan.
4. How long is a bee hummingbird from beak to tail?
   From beak to tail, a bee hummingbird measures 6 centimetres.
5. Which birds have dived to 250 metres?
   Emperor Penguins have dived to 250 metres.

More to think about
true/false/can't tell deductive responses

From what it tells us on the page from the reference book, write in your book 'true', 'false', or 'can't tell' for each of these statements.

1. Ostriches are the biggest birds ever to have lived.   *false*
2. Ostriches are bigger than Emus.   *true*
3. Emperor penguins can't live in shallow water.   *can't tell*
4. Albatrosses can fly faster than buzzards.   *can't tell*
5. Bee hummingbirds only live in jungles.   *can't tell*
6. An ostrich's egg is bigger than that of the African Kori bustard.   *true*
7. The tallest person who ever lived was 2 metres 72 centimetres, more than a metre shorter than the extinct New Zealand Moa.   *true*
8. Cheetahs can run at 100 kilometres per hour, which is faster than the fastest bird can run.   *true*
9. Cheetahs are able to run faster than any bird can fly.   *false*
10. London Zoo has a breeding pair of elephant birds.   *false*

Now try these
incident empathy; vocabulary work

1. Imagine that you could be a record breaker. Write some sentences about which records you would like to break, and say why.
   Notes: *Answers can be shared with others in the class, and can lead to interesting discussions as children justify their reasons.*
2. Words describing size are given.
   a) *Pupils are asked to use a dictionary to help them sort the words into two lists: 'Words meaning big', and 'Words meaning small'.*
      Words meaning big: large, great, bulky, massive, mighty, enormous, huge, colossal
      Words meaning small: minute, tiny, midget, wee, mini, miniature, dwarf, little
3. Take one word from each list and write them in a sentence to show that you know what they mean.

Unit 16 Bus Route

Do you remember?
selecting correct words

Pupils are asked to choose the correct word from two possible choices.

1. The bus starts at the *bottom* of the hill.
2. First it is going into the *town*.
3. In town the bus has to barge through the *traffic*.
4. When it goes into the country the bus is *empty*.
5. The bus goes back into the country to bring more *people* into town.

More to think about
deductive answering in sentences; interpreting language

1. Pupils should write a sentence in their own words to answer each question.
   a) Does the bus route start in the town or in the country?
      The bus starts in the country.

b) Why do you think most people would be travelling?
Most of the passengers are probably travelling into town to work, to go to school, or to go shopping.

c) What lies between the country village and the town?
There is a steep hill between the village and the town.

d) Does the poem suggest whether it is a new or an old bus? How?
It is probably an older bus as the poet describes how it rumbles and rattles.

2. The poet uses some interesting descriptions. Copy into your book how he describes each of these.

a) How the bus, full of passengers, goes up the hill.
'it creeps uphill, like an old man climbing the stairs to bed'

b) What the bus reminds us of as it forces its way through the traffic.
'an angry bull'

c) How the bus seems happier to be out in the country again.
'rattling through the quiet lanes humming softly'

d) What happens to the bus as it squeezes through tight spaces.
'bruise and scrape its skin'

e) How the passengers get onto the bus.
'Swarming crowds of people swarm and clamber on it'

Now try these
character empathy

It is advisable to support most pupils with preliminary discussion if the answers to the first question are not to be superficial, but once the group has empathised with the characters, some extended dialogue can be forthcoming. Also, in pairs pupils can create short playlets, with one being the conductor and the other a passenger of their choice.

1. In your book write ...

a) something the conductor might have said when people were pushing and shoving to get onto the bus.

b) something your mum, loaded with shopping, might have said when it started to rain as she was waiting for the bus, which was late.

c) something you might have said when, one day, the bus was stuck in a snowdrift as you were on your way to school.

2. *Pupils should write sentences in their own words to answer each question.*
Sometimes machines, like Thomas the Tank Engine, can seem almost as though they are human.

a) Do you think the poet thought this bus was like a person? Why?
The poet uses words and phrases that could be used to describe a person, which shows he thinks the bus has some human characteristics.

b) Do you have a machine, like a favourite toy or a bike, that seems to you to have a personality? Write about it.
Notes: *This question asks for pupils to use empathy. Encourage the children to find and collect, and perhaps make an exhibition of, books containing stories and poems based on inanimate objects and animals endowed with human characteristics.*

Unit 17 A Day When Frogs Wear Shoes

Do you remember?
extended cloze from passage

Pupils should note that the following words are missing.
1. *cars* 2. *mile* 3. *Gloria* 4. *Huey* 5. *bored* 6. *Dad*
7. *Ralph's Car Hospital* 8. *three* 9. *bonnet* 10. *hike*

More to think about
deductive answering in sentences

Pupils should write a sentence in their own words to answer each question.

1. Where is the story set?
The story is set on a Caribbean island.

2. Why did Julian usually like visiting his father's workshop?
When Julian visited his dad's workshop the customers made him feel important.

3. How do we know that Julian's father was a positive sort of person?
Julian's father said that the world is such an interesting place nobody should ever be bored.

4. Why was Julian doubtful about going to the workshop on this day?
He thought Huey would give the game away and say that they were bored.

5. Why did they tell Ralph they were off on a hike?
He wanted to get Huey away from the workshop.

6. How can we tell the weather was extremely hot?
Father said that it was so hot that on a day like this, frogs wear shoes.

Now try these
character description; situation empathy

1. Write some sentences to describe these characters from the story. Think carefully before you start, and use the clues in the passage.
a) Julian   b) Huey   c) Ralph, their dad
Notes: *As well as the physical characteristics, encourage the children to speculate about the possible personality traits, and also the relationships which are implied or might be imagined. Children with siblings might be encouraged to explore their feelings about both positive aspects of their relationships with older and younger family members.*

2. Think back to the hottest day you can remember. Write about where you were, what you were doing, and how you felt.
Notes: *This question calls for pupils to use empathy to 'think themselves into' a particular situation and explore their feelings about it.*

Unit 18 Basilisks

Do you remember?
cloze from passage; literal answers in sentences

Copy these sentences. Fill in the missing words.
1. A *cockerel* laid the egg.
2. The egg was kept warm by a *snake*.
3. The basilisk's body was like a *cockerel*.
4. One part of the creature like a snake was its *head*.
5. The only way to kill a basilisk was with a *mirror*.

Pupils should write a sentence in their own words to answer each question.
1. Which part of the basilisk was like a toad?
The basilisk's eyes were like those of a toad.

2. What happened if the basilisk breathed on you?
   If the basilisk breathed on you, you would be killed.
3. Why couldn't a horseman kill the creature?
   The poison would climb up the horseman's spear and kill him and his horse.
4. Where were the two girls found dead?
   The two girls were found in a cellar in Warsaw, in Poland.
5. How did they eventually kill the basilisk in the cellar?
   The basilisk was killed by a criminal dressed in a suit covered in mirrors.

More to think about
interpretation of figurative language

1. Find the words or phrases in the passage that describe:
   a) how the snake moved
      quietly slithered
   b) the basilisk's tongue
      long, forked, darting
   c) what the grass was like
      tall, dark
   d) what the creature's eyes were like
      protruding eyes of a toad
2. The basilisk was said to have 'the protruding eyes of a toad'. Describe the eyes of three people or animals you know. Use good descriptive words.
   Notes: *It is probably better to avoid descriptions of other children in the class!*

Now try these
empathy; retelling myth of choice

1. Write a few sentences describing the different feelings you would have had if you were the criminal told to kill the basilisk.
   Notes: *This question requires pupils to use empathy in order to 'think themselves into' this situation and explore their feelings about it.*
2. The myth of the basilisk is just one of hundreds of monster tales. Retell another monster tale in your book that you know, or make one up.
Notes: *It is possible to plan both of the above activities as class or group work leading to drama opportunities.*

Unit 19 Mrs Wobble the Waitress

Do you remember?
selecting true sentences

Read these sentences about the story. Copy only the ones that are true.
Mrs Wobble has been given the sack.
She keeps dropping the food she is serving.
She is very upset.
Mr Wobble suggests they open a café in their house.
The Wobble children catch the food.
The customers think it is fun.

More to think about
working with phrases; outcome prediction; summarising

1. *Pupils are given groups of words under three columns headed: 'Who?', 'Did what?', 'When?'. They are asked to take a group of words out of each column to make a sensible sentence. Their sentences should be:*
   Mrs Wobble was very upset when she lost her job.
   Mr Wobble had an idea when he saw Mrs Wobble crying.
   Miss Wobble skated to the rescue to catch the soup
   Master Wobble skated to the rescue to catch the chicken.
   The customers cheered as they watched the excitement.

2. Write a few sentences to tell how you think the story might finish. Try to make it interesting or funny.
   Notes: *This requires pupils to have understood the story in order to predict possible outcomes. Choose other, similar stories to be read aloud to the class.*
3. Write a summary of the story of *Mrs Wobble the Waitress* in your own words. Try not to use more than 40 words.
   Notes: *This summary writing can be difficult for some pupils. Support can be given by initial discussion with the class or in groups to isolate the main idea and key events.*

Now try these
critical evaluation of content

This is a funny story, but kitchens can be dangerous places.
1. Make a list of possible dangers in a kitchen.
2. Write a set of rules to help to make your kitchen at home a safer place.
   Notes: *The first two questions require pupils to draw on experience outside the text.*
3. Do you think writers should write funny stories about serious things? Give your reasons.
   Notes: *This question builds on the previous two in asking pupils to make judgements based on their outside experience. The first two questions can be developed further by allowing selected children to prepare wall posters, the stated objectives of which are to educate and persuade.*

Unit 20 Humans – Friend or Foe?

Do you remember?
selecting correct answers

Select the correct answer from two possible choices.
1. Who painted the picture?
   a) The picture was painted by Todi Ragini, from India.
2. Who wrote the poem?
   b) The poem was written by an unknown poet from Africa.
3. Is the woman in the picture a friend or an enemy of the creatures?
   a) The woman is a friend of the creatures.
4. Are the people in the poem kind to the animals?
   a) No, the poem is about people who want to hunt the animals.

More to think about
deductive answering in sentences

Pupils should write a sentence in their own words to answer each question.
1. Do you think the woman in the picture is poor or wealthy. How can you tell?
   The woman looks to be well dressed and is probably wealthy.
2. Why are the deer following her?
   The deer are following her as they may expect her to feed them.
3. What is it about the animals that show they think they can trust the woman?
   The deer are all following closely without any hesitation.
4. What words does the poet use to suggest that antelopes are timid creatures?
   The poet writes of the antelope 'stepping cautiously'.
5. The poet compares the antelope's eyes to those of birds. What other similarities can you think of between deer and antelope and any other creatures?
   Notes: *This question encourages pupils to deduce similarities from what they know.*

Book 2

Now try these
arguing a case

Deer hunting has been banned in some countries.
Do you think deer hunting is cruel and should be banned, or
should hunters be allowed to hunt deer for food?
Write about what you think.

Notes: *This task is best conducted initially as a class activity,
with the children suggesting the pros and cons and you
listing them under appropriate headings on a board. The
children should then refer to this as they write their own
version of an argument either in favour of or against hunting.
A similar approach might be taken to considering arguments
around other contentious issues, especially school-based or
other local community issues, such as a new road proposal,
a supermarket development, the closing of a local library.*

Progress Unit B

Do you remember?
sentence completion; literal answers in sentences
*Score: 1 mark for each correct answer except where shown
otherwise (maximum 12 marks).*

Notes: *Ensure the children realise that the first group of
questions relates to the prose extract, whereas the second
relates to the poem. Pupils are asked to write endings to the
sentences about Arthur.*

1. Not being allowed to watch TV makes Arthur *(very, very,)
angry.*
2. His mother said he must *control his anger. (2 marks,
'get angry' is also acceptable for 1 mark)*
3. His anger was at first like *a storm cloud (exploding
thunder and lightning and hailstones).*
4. Then it became like a hurricane hurling *rooftops and
chimneys and church spires.*
5. In the end he couldn't remember why *he was so angry.
(2 marks)*

*Pupils should write a sentence in their own words to answer
each question about Bertie*

1. Who was he angry with?
   Bertie was angry with his brother.
2. Why was he so cross?
   *He was angry because his brother had kicked his ball over
   the fence.*
3. Which parts of his body did his anger affect?
   *His anger affected his eyes, nose, mouth, stomach, fists,
   head and feet. (score one mark if five or more are listed.)*
4. Did he manage to control his temper?
   No, Bertie didn't control his anger. (2 marks)

More to think about
interpretation of figurative language
*Score: Q1 award up to 2 marks; Q2 1 mark for each correct
answer; Q3 up to 3 marks (maximum 7 marks).*

1. Haiwyn Oram, the author of *Angry Arthur*, says Arthur's
   anger becomes other things. How can we tell that he is
   getting more and more angry as the story goes on?
   *Answers should refer to the growing scale of the
   devastation described in the passage.*

2. Copy the similes Bertie uses to describe:
   a) how his eyes feel   *like fried eggs in a pan*
   b) how his breathing is affected   *like a dragon*
   c) how he is holding his hands   *like compressing a
   lemon*
3. Which phrase tells us that in the end Bertie actually lost
   his temper?
   And then I burst out.

Now try these
character empathy

*Score: the marks awarded in this section are discretionary,
according to the judgement of the teacher. The pieces need
not be awarded marks individually; what is significant is the
extent to which the child is beginning to empathise, and to
demonstrate evaluative and appreciative skills. For this
reason an alternative to asking for all the questions to be
completed is for the child to be allowed to select just one or
two tasks from the five, and for these to be worked on in
more depth. Marks towards the higher end of the scale
should also be reserved for those presenting their work in
well constructed, and appropriately punctuated sentences
(maximum 11 marks).*

*Pupils should write a sentence in their own words to answer
each question.*

1. Do you think either Arthur or Bertie were right to feel as
   angry as they did? Why?
2. Do you feel sorry for Arthur or Bertie or both of them?
   Why?
3. Which of the two pieces of writing is the better description
   of someone getting really angry? Say why you think this.
4. Should we always try to control our anger, or should we
   sometimes allow ourselves to show our anger? Give
   reasons for your answer, and give some examples when it
   is probably better to control our feelings of anger.
5. Think of an occasion when you felt really angry. Why were
   you so cross? How did it make you feel? What happened
   in the end?

Indicative scores for National Curriculum

Below level 2	Level 2	Level 3	Level 4
0-4	5-14	15-26	27-30

Indicative scores for 5–14 Guidelines

Level A	Level B	Level C
0-5	6-18	19-30

Book 3

Scope and sequence of skills

Unit	Title	Page	Do you remember? *Reading the lines*	More to think about *Reading between the lines*	Now try these *Reading beyond the lines*
1	**Fascinating Animal Facts** *Information book extract*	4	cloze from passage	deductive answering in sentences	vocabulary work; deductive sentence completion
2	**The Big Match** *Modern poem*	6	literal answering in sentences	figurative language; deductive answering in sentences; outcome prediction	empathy
3	**A Clever Way to Catch a Thief** *Text from other cultures*	8	selecting appropriate endings	matching questions to answers	evaluation and projection; vocabulary work; review
4	**The Invisible Dog** *Modern fiction*	11	selecting correct answers; literal answering in sentences	deductive answering in sentences; character deduction	vocabulary work; character empathy; story completion
5	**The Donkey** *Classic poem*	14	word selection	figurative language	vocabulary/dictionary work; lists – assessing and evaluating; review
6	**Magic Matchsticks** *Instructions*	16	cloze	sequencing sentences; writing instructions	vocabulary work; empathy
7	**The Shark** *Classic poem*	19	cloze	deductive answering in sentences; summarising in newspaper style	vocabulary/dictionary work; character empathy; review
8	**Noisy Neighbours** *Business letter*	22	selecting correct answers	deductive answering in sentences	vocabulary enrichment; appreciative responses

Book 3

Unit 1 Fascinating Animal Facts

Do you remember?
cloze from passage

1. When fish sleep their *bodies* slow down.
2. The slippery sides of a bath make it *(almost) impossible* for a spider to climb out.
3. Bats have special *claws* to help them hang upside down.
4. Budgies' feet are naturally *clenched* when they sleep.
5. An *elephant* has large ears to help to keep it cool.
6. Fish swim in shoals to *protect* themselves from attack.

More to think about
deductive answering in sentences

Pupils should write a sentence in their own words to answer each question.

1. Do spiders get into baths by coming up the plug hole?
   No, they fall into the bath and then find it almost impossible to climb out.
2. Why might it be unsafe for bats to roost on the ground?
   If bats roosted on the ground they might be attacked.
3. How can we tell that birds naturally clench their feet?
   If a dead bird is examined its feet are naturally clenched.

4. Give three reasons why fish often swim in shoals.
   Fish swim in shoals to protect themselves from predators during the spawning season and also to make it easier to move through the water.
5. What happens to a fish's brain pattern when it sleeps?
   When a fish sleeps its brainwaves remain the same as when it is awake.

Now try these
vocabulary work; deductive sentence completion
1. Find a word or phrase in one of the passages that means the same as:
   a) the place where fish live   *their environment*
   b) to hang upside down   *to hang in an inverted position*
   c) gripping firmly   *clenching*
   d) very large   *enormous*
   e) creatures likely to attack other creatures   *predators*
2. Think of a sensible ending for each of these sentences.
   Pupils are instructed that it may be useful to use a reference book to check their answers.
   a) Giraffes evolved with long necks so that *they can reach otherwise inaccessible food high above the ground.*
   b) Some people think wolves howl at the moon because *they are nocturnal creatures.*
   c) We know what dinosaurs looked like by *examining their fossil remains.*
   d) Tigers have stripes to *improve their camouflage in their natural habitat of grasslands.*
   e) Cactuses have thorns to prevent *them from being eaten by animals.*
   Notes: *Note taking from information books is an important, but difficult, skill to master. Frequent work on identifying the main idea in a section or paragraph can be productive, and to this end a selection of photocopied pages which the children mark with highlighter pens can be a useful way of extending this unit.*

Unit 2 The Big Match

Do you remember?
literal answering in sentences
Pupils should write a sentence in their own words to answer each question.
1. Which two teams were playing the match?
   The match was being played between Danebridge and Shenby school teams.
2. Who was Danebridge's goal-keeper?
   Chris was Danebridge's goal-keeper.
3. Who was Danebridge's captain?
   Danebridge's captain was Tim.
4. Why was it a bad day for Duggan?
   He gave away a penalty.
5. Who took the penalty?
   The penalty was taken by the Shenby captain.

More to think about
figurative language; deductive answering in sentences; outcome prediction
1. Find these phrases in the passage, and write them in your own words.
   a) when disaster strikes   *when something serious unexpectedly happens*
   b) a great ruck of bodies   *a large group pushing and shoving*
   c) both goals survived narrow squeaks   *both teams came close to scoring*

d) rescue the situation   *prevent things going wrong*
   e) Time was rapidly running out   *the game was nearly over*
   f) hushed in anticipation   *waiting very quietly*
   g) their slender lead   *they were only just ahead*
   h) hoping for a miracle   *hoping something almost impossible might happen*
2. *Pupils should write a sentence in their own words to answer each question.*
   a) Why was it an important match?
      It was a cup match.
   b) Why did Duggan touch the ball?
      He did it in panic, without thinking properly.
   c) How do we know Duggan was deeply upset?
      He slumped to the ground in distress.
   d) Why did some of the players hardly dare to watch when the penalty was being taken?
      They knew that if the penalty was scored, Danebridge would have lost their lead, just when they thought they had almost won the match.
3. Write a few sentences describing how you imagine the story finishes.
   Notes: *There are limited options in terms of the score. What is more interesting and significant is how the result, whatever the child chooses it to be, impacts on the characters in the story.*

Now try these
empathy
1. How would you have felt, and what thoughts would have been going through your mind, if you were:
   a) Duggan   b) Chris   c) Grandad
   d) the Shenby team captain
   Notes: *This question requires pupils to show empathy towards the different characters, entering into their situations and considering their personal characteristics.*
2. Duggan and Chris loved football; it was their favourite game. Do you have a favourite sport? Give your reasons. If you don't like any sports or games say why.
   Again this question calls for pupils to use empathy to explore their own feelings.
Notes: *Either or both activities in this section could, for variety, be presented as a letter to a friend or relative.*

Unit 3 A Clever Way to Catch a Thief

Do you remember?
selecting appropriate endings
Pupils should select the most appropriate endings from two possible choices.
1. The rich man thought his things were being stolen by
   b) one of his servants
2. The servants were
   a) sorry to think one of them was untrustworthy.
3. The rich man told his servants to
   b) go one at a time into the darkened room.
4. Inside the room there was
   a) an empty box on the table.
5. The box was
   b) covered in black soot.

Book 3

More to think about
matching questions to answers

1. *Pupils should write a question in their own words to go with each answer. The first one has been done for pupils, as an example.*
   a) The story takes place in the West Indies.
      Where does the story take place?
   b) The rich man realised some of his things had been stolen.
      Why did the rich man suspect one of his servants of stealing?
   c) He made each servant in turn go into the darkened room and touch the box.
      What did he tell each of his servants to do?
   d) Not a sound was heard in the room.
      What happened when each of them went into the room?
   e) There was nothing in the box.
      What was actually in the box on the table?
   f) The servant with the clean hand was guilty.
      How could the rich man tell which of his servants was guilty?

2. Write a brief version of the story in not more than 40 words.
   Notes: *Suggest that the children might start this activity by*
   a) identifying the main idea, and
   b) noting the key words or phrases in each paragraph.

Now try these
evaluation and projection; vocabulary work; review

1. *Pupils should write a sentence in their own words to answer each question.*
   a) This story took place many years ago. Do you think this method of detection would work now? Say why.
      This question calls for pupils to evaluate content in terms of knowledge and experience drawn from outside the text.
   b) If this story were to happen now, and you were a police officer, how would you set about solving the crime?
      This question builds on the previous question and requires pupils to, in addition, project themselves into the situation and consider what they might do.

2. Copy these lists next to each other in your book. Draw a line between the words or phrases that have similar meanings.
   The first one has been done for pupils, as an example.
   The following connections should be made:
   detect *find out*; culprit *guilty person*; perplexed *puzzled*; guilty *committed an offence*; immediately *straight away*; anxious *uneasy*; innocent *not guilty*; thrusting *pushing*; exclaimed *cried out*

3. Did you enjoy reading this short story? Write a few sentences describing to a friend who hasn't read the story what you think they would like most about it, or what they might not like about it.
   Notes: *An alternative way of presenting this activity is to suggest the children imagine that they are writing a review for a newspaper.*

Unit 4 The Invisible Dog

Do you remember?
selecting correct answers; literal answering in sentences
Pupils should select the correct answer from two possible choices.
1. Who was Rupert?   *a) Rupert was a pet dog.*
2. What type of dog was Rupert?   *a) He was a Great Dane.*
3. How old was Janie when Rupert died?
   b) Janie was two when Rupert died.
4. How old was Rupert when he died?
   a) Rupert died when he was eight.
5. What did Janie find that reminded her of the dog?
   b) Janie found his collar.
6. Pupils should write a sentence in their own words to answer each question.
   a) Where did Janie find Rupert's collar?
      Janie found the collar in the garage.
   b) What was the collar like?
      The collar was big, broad and brass-studded, with a round metal disc attached to the buckle.
   c) How did she know it was Rupert's old collar?
      Rupert's name was scratched on the disc.
   d) Why did she feel sad when she first found the collar?
      She was sad that the faint smell was all that was left of Rupert.
   e) What did she imagine as she walked along the lane holding the collar?
      She imagined that she was walking Rupert.

More to think about
deductive answering in sentences; character deduction
1. Read the passage again carefully. Write some sentences about:
   a) why you think the story is called 'The Invisible Dog'.
      Rupert is very real, but only in Janie's imagination.
   b) what facts you can find out about Janie.
      Answers should refer to her inquisitiveness, strong imagination; liking for animals; that she lived in a village.
   c) what facts you can find out about Mrs Garrow.
      Answers should refer to her friendliness, that she was an elderly widow and lived alone, that she had a loud laugh that sounded like a duck quacking, that she liked animals, lived in a village, and had a strong imagination.
2. Use the facts that you have discovered as well as your imagination to write a word picture of Mrs Garrow.
   Notes: *This question calls for pupils to make deductions about Mrs Garrow's character.*

Now try these
vocabulary work; character empathy; story completion
1. Which word or phrase in each list means the same as the word in bold letters?
   Pupils are asked to select from five possible choices.
   a) often *frequently*   b) attached *joined*
   c) encircle *surround*   d) circlet *small circle*
   e) pacing *walking*
2. Pretending can be fun. Janie pretended she had a dog. Imagine you could choose any pet as a present.
   a) Say what you would choose, and why.
   b) Explain what preparations you might need to make before your new pet arrives.
   c) Describe how you would look after it.
   Notes: *This question calls for pupils to use their imaginations in order to empathise.*

3. When Janie first found the lead she felt sad. Write about a time when you felt sad about something. Describe your feelings, and say if anything helped you to feel better.
   Notes: *This activity might touch some sensitive nerves f or some children, and individual teachers will make judgements about how to handle children who may recently have suffered serious trauma, such as bereavement or family break-up. In some instances, being able to write about or talk about the events can be therapeutic.*

4. Write a few sentences explaining what you think might have happened at the end of the story of 'The Invisible Dog'.
   This question calls for pupils to use their imaginations to complete the story.

Unit 5 The Donkey

Do you remember?
word selection

Pupils should select the correct answers from three possible choices.
1. How old was the donkey?   *a) one day*
2. What were his legs like?   *b) shaky*
3. What did he do when he stood up?   *b) tried to gambol*
4. What did his face look like?   *c) wistful*
5. How did he lie on the ground to rest?   *a) flat*

More to think about
figurative language

1. Write in your book the words that are used to describe:
   a) the donkey's legs
      His legs were shaky and long and loose,
      They rocked and staggered and weren't much use.
   b) how he tried to move
      He tried to gambol and frisk a bit
   c) what his coat was like
      Was soft and grey and curled at his neck
   d) the expression on his face
      wistful
2. The poet has described a small donkey. Now think of the words and phrases you might use to describe these features of a bull.
   a) his legs   b) how he moves   c) his coat
   d) the expression on his face.
   Notes: *Having something concrete to discuss and write about helps the development of vocabulary, and an exercise of this type can usefully become a regular part of the language work of the class.*

Now try these
vocabulary/dictionary work; lists – assessing and evaluating; review

1. What do these words mean? Use a dictionary to help you.
   a) gambol *v. to jump about; n. a frolic*
   b) wistful *adj. longing, yearning*
   c) blundered *v. to have moved clumsily*
   d) venturesome *adj. daring*
   e) quest *n. search*
   Notes: *Regular dictionary practice at this stage is vital. Use this opportunity for a class session on the structure of entries in a dictionary, and the meaning of the abbreviations.*

2. Do you think it would be nice to live on a farm? Make two lists showing four good things and four bad things.
   Notes: *This question requires pupils to assess and*

evaluate items in order to make lists. The first one on each list has been done for them, as an example.

3. If you were to give marks out of ten to this poem, how many would you give it? Why?
   Notes: *Children should be encouraged to express opinions and criticise the poetry and prose they are offered. An extension of this activity is to set up a kind of 'Eurovision Song Contest', with two or three poems read, followed by group discussions in which each group decides a mark for each poem. These can be collected together and a 'favourite poem of the week' announced.*

Unit 6 Magic Matchsticks

Do you remember?
cloze

Choose a word from the box to fill each gap. Write the missing words in your book.
1. *tricks*   2. *rabbits*   3. *hats*   4. *women*   5. *magician*
6. *practise*   7. *thoroughly*   8. *work*   9. *audience*
10. *embarrassed*

More to think about
sequencing sentences; writing instructions

1. The sentences should be ordered as follows:
   Collect together a handkerchief and some matchsticks.
   Rehearse the trick thoroughly.
   Show the audience a matchstick.
   Show the audience the handkerchief.
   Wrap the matchstick in the handkerchief.
   Ask someone to break the matchstick in the handkerchief.
   Open the handkerchief and show the unbroken matchstick.
2. Do you know a magic trick? If you do, write the instructions step by step like those for the matchstick trick. If you don't, write instructions to teach a young child how to cross a busy road.
   Notes: *This question calls for pupils to write clear and simple instructions.*

Now try these
vocabulary work; empathy

1. *Pupils are asked to find words in the passage which mean the same as the following (they are told which paragraph the word is in):*
   a) fascinated *intrigued*   b) not possible *impossible*
   c) practising *rehearsing*   d) hidden *secreted*
   e) amazed *flabbergasted*   f) doubtful *suspicious*
2. Imagine that you really do have a magic wand. You can use it to change three things, but three things only! Write in your book what you will change, and say why.
   Notes: *The opportunity to change the world is something we all relish. Pupils may produce some weird and wonderful answers as well as some rather pedestrian ones. The important dimension to be stressed in this context is the reasons pupils give for their answers, and how well and concisely they are set out. This activity may usefully be extended by illustrating ideas through artwork. This can be attractively displayed alongside pupils' written work.*

Unit 7 The Shark

Do you remember?
cloze

1. The poem is about a *shark*.
2. He watches as the boy takes off his *clothes*.
3. He pretends to take no *notice*.
4. The shark even pretends that he's *asleep*.
5. Then suddenly he throws his *body* about.
6. You can then see he has a black *back*.
7. He has a white *stomach*.
8. He has a very dangerous *bite*.

More to think about
deductive answering in sentences; summarising in newspaper style

1. Write a sentence to answer each question.
   a) Why are sharks said to be treacherous?
      Sharks are treacherous because they appear not to be particularly dangerous, but can suddenly and unexpectedly attack.
   b) Explain why the poet says the shark has 'astounding self-control'.
      The shark will wait patiently until its prey is very close before making its attack.
   c) Why does the shark pretend to be asleep as the boy runs down to the sea?
      The shark is lulling the boy into a false sense of security.
   d) What is the 'true character' of the shark?
      The shark is not the placid, gentle creature it appears, but a dangerous and aggressive one.
   e) Is this poem fair to all sharks? Give your reasons.
      No, for although some sharks are aggressive towards people, most are quite harmless.
2. Rewrite the poem as if it were an article for a newspaper. The poem doesn't tell us what happened in the end, but your article should.
   Notes: *This question calls for pupils to summarise the information given in the poem in the style of newspaper reporting.*

Now try these
vocabulary/dictionary work; character empathy; review

1. Write these phrases in another way. Use a dictionary to help you.
   a) a treacherous monster
      a dangerously unreliable creature
   b) never makes the least remark
      never makes any sound
   c) not the least excitement shows
      doesn't get excited
   d) astounding self-control
      able to control his emotions and reactions
   e) his whole demeanour
      his outward behaviour and attitude
   f) throws his body right about
      goes into the attack
   g) his true character
      his real personality
   h) all decent feeling
      all sympathy or kindness
2. Write one-word answers to these questions in your book.
   a) One word in the poem is not spelt as we would spell it now. Which word is it?   *undrest (undressed)*
   b) Which word rhymes with sand?   *land*
   c) Which word rhymes with asleep?   *leap*
   d) Which word rhymes with change?   *range*
   e) Which word rhymes with appealing?   *feeling*

3. Imagine that you were the shark in the poem. Tell the story in your own words, from the shark's point of view. Start when you are basking in the warmth of the sun, and suddenly you spot…
   Notes: *Preliminary group or class work will stimulate better responses. The key is to encourage the children to think themselves into the world of the shark and its physical and social environment, its need to survive and to support its young and so on. Discuss and list possible vocabulary options before the work commences.*
4. What would you say to your friends to encourage them to read this poem?
   Notes: *You will notice that, increasingly now, pupils are being encouraged to express an opinion about whether and why they like/dislike the passages. This is an important step in encouraging their growth as discerning readers.*

Unit 8 Noisy Neighbours

Do you remember?
selecting correct answers

Pupils are asked to select the correct answer from two possible choices.

1. Who is the letter from?
   a) The letter is from the Complaints Officer of Southborough Council.
2. What is the Complaints Officer's name?
   b) The Complaints Officer is Mr B Quiet.
3. When was the letter sent?
   a) The letter was sent on 1st October.
4. What is the letter about?
   a) It is about the noise coming from Mr Trigger's flat.
5. Is this the first letter sent to Mr Trigger about noise?
   b) No, there have been other letters sent to him.
6. What happened when the last letter was sent?
   b) Nothing changed when the last letter was sent.
7. What will happen if this letter is ignored?
   a) The Council will take Mr Trigger to court if he ignores this letter.

More to think about
deductive answering in sentences

Pupils should write a sentence in their own words to answer each question.

1. How many letters has Mr Quiet sent to Mr Trigger?
   This is the third letter to be sent.
2. How did Mr Quiet know a lot of noise was coming from Mr Trigger's flat?
   There had been continuing complaints from Mr Trigger's neighbours.
3. Why is Mr Quiet particularly cross with Mr Trigger?
   Although Mr Trigger promised to keep his family quieter, the problem hasn't changed.
4. Does Mr Trigger live alone in the flat?
   No, he lives in the flat with his family.
5. What are the main causes of the noise?
   Most of the noise comes from the stereo, the dogs, a violin and various household appliances.
6. What will happen if the noise is not reduced?
   If the noise isn't reduced Mr Trigger will be prosecuted.

Now try these
vocabulary enrichment; appreciative responses

1. *Pupils are given a list of words from the passage together with a list of meanings. They are asked to match words from the passage to their correct meanings. The first one has been done for them, as an example.*
   emanating *coming from*; occasion *time*; assured *promised*; cease *stop*; forthwith *immediately*; agonising *awful*; incessantly *constantly*; restrain *prevent*; disregard *lack of consideration*; distraught *extremely agitated*.

2. Write in your book a few sentences to answer each of these questions.
   a) It's a free country, so do you think people should be allowed to make as much noise as they want? Give reasons for your answer.
   b) Has anyone ever really annoyed you in some way? What was the reason, and how was it sorted out?
   c) What things should people be most aware of to prevent upsetting their neighbours?
   Notes: *As an extension, 2a) can be developed into a class debate. Careful preparation is required to ensure that the arguments on both sides are properly marshalled and presented. This can be done with two groups debating against each other, after which the rest of the class can vote (possibly through a secret ballot) to show which side of the argument got most support. Questions 2b) and 2c) encourage pupils to consider viewpoints from all sides in ways which are constructive.*

Unit 9 The Two Brothers

Do you remember?
true/false/can't tell literal responses

1. Write in your book 'true', 'false', or 'can't tell' for each one.
   a) The story is about two brothers. *true*
   b) The story is set in America. *false*
   c) The older brother is braver than the younger. *false*
   d) They found a tiny old lady in the trunk of a tree. *false*
   e) She was over 100 years old. *can't tell*
   f) It was hot, and the boys became thirsty. *true*
   g) There was a stream at the bottom of the ravine. *true*
   h) The younger brother trapped his older brother in the ravine. *false*
   i) A honey-bird led the boys' father to the spot. *true*
   j) In the end, the two brothers lived together happily. *false*

2. *Pupils are asked to select from two possible choices the correct words to end each sentence.*
   a) The two brothers went *hunting*.
   b) They found a circle of *pots*.
   c) The old lady led the younger brother to a *tree*.
   d) Inside the trunk were many *animals*.
   e) The brothers started to drive the animals back to the *village*.

More to think about
deductive answering in sentences; summarising

1. *Pupils should write a sentence in their own words to answer each question.*
   a) Why did the older brother not want to touch the circle of pots?
      The older brother said that he got a bad feeling about the pots.
   b) Who was the braver of the two brothers?
      The younger brother was the braver brother.

c) How can we tell that the old woman wasn't frightened of the boys?
   As soon as she was released she shouted orders at the boys.
d) Why did the woman give the younger brother all the animals?
   She gave the younger brother the animals because he had released her.
e) How do we know it was probably the hot, dry season?
   The story refers to the dusty tracks and the boys becoming increasingly thirsty.
f) Why wasn't the brothers' mother concerned when the younger brother failed to return with the older brother?
   The older brother lied to her that the younger brother would be returning in a few days.
g) Why did the younger brother give the honey-bird seed and water everyday?
   He believed it was the bird that had saved his life.
h) What do you think became of the old woman?
   Possibly the honey-bird was the spirit of the old woman.

2. Write a summary of the story of the 'Two Brothers' in your own words. Don't use more than 60 words.
   Notes: *By this stage it is helpful to remove the passage before the exercise of summarising is undertaken. However, while the book is still open, encourage the pupils to think about the key ideas in the passage.*

Now try these
vocabulary work; character/setting analysis; review

1. Find these words in the passage. Write another word or phrase that the author could have used without changing the meaning.
   a) begged *pleaded/beseeched*
   b) rigid *unable to move/rooted to the spot*
   c) commanded *demanded*
   d) ravine *steep-sided, deep valley*
   e) incredible *amazing/unbelievable*
   f) occasionally *from time to time*
   g) precipice *cliff*
   h) fashioned *made*

2. Use the clues in the story, and your imagination, to write short word-pictures to describe the personalities of these main characters:
   a) the younger brother   b) the older brother
   c) the old lady   d) the boys' father.
   This question calls for pupils to analyse the different characters in the passage.

3. What do you think would be the best things about living in an African village like the one in the story? The worst things? Make two lists.
   Notes: *Initially pupils may be able to deduce some of their answers from the text and other sources previously encountered. However, the work might be extended for some by asking them to undertake research in library books and encyclopaedia.*

4. Write about whether you enjoyed the story. How did it make you feel? What parts did you like most? Did you like the way it was written?
   Notes: *This question calls for pupils to review the text, exploring their feelings and giving persuasive reasons for the judgements they make about it.*

Unit 10 The Borrowers

Do you remember?
literal answering in sentences; selecting true statements

1. Pupils should write a sentence in their own words to answer each question.
   a) Who are the Borrowers?
      The Borrowers are a race of tiny people.
   b) Where do they live?
      They live, hidden, in houses or wherever they can find a safe convenient place.
   c) What were Mrs May and Kate making?
      Mrs May and Kate were making a bed-quilt.
   d) What had Kate lost?
      Kate had lost her crochet hook.
   e) Where did she think she had put the crochet hook?
      She thought that she had left it on the bottom shelf of the book case.

2. Read these sentences about the story. Copy only the ones that are true.
   The crochet hook was missing, but the wool was still there.
   Their name for people was 'human beans'.
   The little people collected things like pencils, hair slides, drawing pins.
   Mrs May knew someone who had met the Borrowers.

More to think about
deductive answering in sentences and lists

1. Pupils should write a sentence in their own words to answer each question.
   a) Why was the race of little people called the Borrowers?
      The little people became known as the Borrowers because they borrowed all their implements from humans.
   b) Why did the Borrowers call people 'human beans'?
      Human beans sounds like human beings.
   c) What time of the day, and at what time of the year, is the story probably taking place? How can you tell?
      As they were working by a fire in the half-light, it was probably an autumn or winter afternoon.
   d) How did Kate feel when Mrs May first mentioned the Borrowers?
      Kate was at first a little fearful at the idea that Borrowers might exist.
   e) Why did Kate begin to feel impatient with Mrs May?
      Kate grew impatient with Mrs May when it became clear that she was withholding information from her about the Borrowers.

2. Make a list of the clues in the passage that tell us The Borrowers was written about 50 years ago.
   Answers might include: crochet hooks; shoes with buttons; sealing wax; hat pins; blotting paper.

Now try these
evaluating reality and fantasy; character empathy

1. Whenever strange things happen people look for reasons. Do you think it is possible that there could be, or could ever have been, a race of tiny people like the Borrowers? Give your reasons.
   Notes: *This question calls for pupils to make judgements about what is 'real' and what is fantastic. The reasons pupils give will be important here.*

2. Imagine that you were accidentally given a spoonful of medicine that had the unexpected effect of shrinking you. Write about some of the dangers, but also about some of the things you could do if you were tiny that you can't do at your usual size.

Notes: *In discussion, parallels may be drawn between the little people in The Borrowers and the Lilliputians in Gulliver's Travels, which is used in Unit 10 in Book 4*

3. Does this passage from 'The Borrowers' make you feel you would like to read the whole book? Give your reasons.
   Notes: *This question calls for pupils to evaluate the passage and persuasively justify the judgement they make.*

Progress Unit A

Do you remember?
sentence completion

Score: 1 mark for each correct answer to questions 1-3; 2 marks for each correct answer to questions 4-6 (maximum 9 marks).

Think of sensible words from the passage to finish these sentences.
1. Wendy was afraid of *Simon McTavish.*
2. Her teacher was *Mrs Paterson.*
3. Mrs Paterson had her best ideas *in the bath.*
4. She thought for Parents' Evening her class could hold an *exhibition of 'Interesting things'.*
5. Wendy said she could bring her *grandad's old war helmet.*
6. When Simon McTavish was rude Wendy *felt the tears coming.*

More to think about
character analysis

Score: 3 marks for each correct answer (maximum 12 marks).

Pupils should write a few sentences in their own words to answer each question.
1. What sort of person was Simon McTavish? Why do you think this?
   Answers should refer to his restlessness, arrogance/ rudeness, potential bullying tendencies.
2. How do we know that Wendy was afraid of him?
   Wendy tried to avoid him in the playground, and through the day she would keep watching him.
3. Why did Wendy like her teacher?
   Wendy liked her teacher because she laughed a lot.
4. If you were Mrs Paterson, how would you have felt about Simon McTavish?
   Answers should refer to his rudeness and disruptive behaviour.

Now try these
story completion; character empathy

Score: the marks awarded in this section are discretionary, according to your judgement. The pieces need not be awarded marks individually; what is significant is the extent to which the child is beginning to predict and to empathise. For this reason an alternative to asking for all the questions to be completed is for the child to be allowed to select just one or two tasks, and for these to be worked on in more depth. Marks towards the higher end of the scale should be reserved for those presenting their work in well constructed, and appropriately punctuated sentences (maximum 9 marks).

1. What do you think happened in the end? Make up your own ending for this story.
2. If you were being threatened or bullied, write in your book what each of these people would say if you told them:
   a) your teacher   b) your mum   c) your grandad
   d) your best friend.

3. Write in your book how you would feel, and what you would do, if:
   a) your younger brother or sister was being bullied
   b) your best friend was frightened of a gang in the playground.

Indicative scores for National Curriculum

Below level 2	Level 2	Level 3	Level 4
0-4	5-17	18-25	26-30

Indicative scores for 5–14 Guidelines

Level A	Level B	Level C	Level D
0-4	5-14	15-24	25-30

Unit 11 Around and Around it goes

Do you remember?
selecting the correct answers

Pupils are asked to select the correct answer from two possible choices.

1. What is water that has become solid?
   a) *Water that has become solid is ice.*
2. How much of the Earth is covered by water?
   a) *Three quarters of the Earth is covered by water.*
3. What happens when the sea is warmed by the sun?
   b) *Some water turns into water vapour.*
4. What happens to the water vapour?
   a) *The water vapour turns into clouds and rain.*
5. Where does most of the rain go?
   a) *Most of the rain finds its way into rivers that flow back to the sea.*

More to think about
sequencing; deductive answering in sentences

1. *The sentences should be sequenced as follows:*
   Warmed water turns into water vapour and rises into the sky.
   As the water vapour cools it turns into clouds.
   The clouds drift over the land.
   Rain falls from the clouds.
   The water seeps through the soil and back into rivers.
   The rivers take the water back to the sea.
2. Pupils should write a sentence in their own words to answer each question.
   a) Why is this process called 'the water cycle'?
      It is called the water cycle because the water goes around and around.
   b) Why is there usually more rain on the hills near the coast of large land areas than there is in their centres?
      Most of the moisture falls from the clouds when they first rise over the hills, leaving less moisture to fall from them as they move inland.
   c) Is there usually more rain if the wind is blowing towards the land or towards the sea?
      There is more rain if the wind is blowing across the sea and towards the land.
   d) What would the weather be like on land if the wind was blowing the clouds away from the land and out to sea?
      The weather would be dry.
   e) What causes a river to flood?
      Rivers flood when the rainfall is heavier than usual and all the water won't fit between the banks of the river.

Now try these
deductive answering in sentences; factual evaluation

1. What do these weather words mean? Use a dictionary to help you.
   a) precipitation   *rain, snow or hail, falling to the ground*
   b) cyclone   *a system of winds*
   c) evaporation   *liquid turning into vapour*
   d) drought   *lack of rain for a period*
   e) drizzle   *light, misty rain*
   f) storm   *severe weather, strong winds and usually heavy rain or snow*
2. Why would life on Earth be impossible without water?
   Pupils should refer to our fundamental need for water to drink, to grow crops for food, for our animals to survive, for trees to grow (timber) etc. You can compare this with nearby planets (such as Mars) which have no water.
3. Why are we sometimes short of water for our taps? What are the main problems for people when there is a shortage of water? What sorts of people suffer most?
   Pupils may refer to a) lack of rainfall b) difficulties caused - water for bathing, washing clothes, toilets (for work places, especially factories), horticulture, agriculture and gardens c) people who need/use water in the above contexts.

Notes: *Extension work can lead into environmental considerations of water conservation, and the problems that arise when too much water is extracted from rivers and ground-water supplies.*

Unit 12 Ou and Ouch

Do you remember?
cloze from passage

Pupils should note that the following words are missing:
1. *wealthy* 2. *miserly* 3. *workers* 4. *lad* 5. *month*
6. *Ou* 7. *Ouch* 8. *jars* 9. *mouse* 10. *rat*

More to think about
reconstructing sentences; character description; summarising

1. *Pupils are given groups of words under three columns, headed: 'Who?', 'Does what?', 'When?'. They are asked to take a group of words out of each column to make a sensible sentence. Their sentences should be:*
   The farmer never paid his workers at the end of the month.
   The lad thought of a clever plan when the farmer sent him to market.
   The men watched the lad when he returned with the jars.
2. In the first paragraph of the actual story there are two words that tell us what sort of person the farmer was. Write the words in your book, and say what they mean.
   wealthy *rich;* miserly *mean with his money*
3. Copy other words the writer uses in the passage to give us clues about the character of the farmer.
   up to no good; stingy; wizen-faced; gruff; grumpy; old
4. Write a brief version of the story using your own words. Use no more than 40 words.
   Notes: *If possible, pupils should by now be trying to summarise without recourse to the passage.*

Now try these
evaluating titles; incident empathy

1. Do you think 'Ou and Ouch' is a good title? Make a list of other possible titles, neatly underlining your favourite.

2. Did you enjoy the story? Write about why you think it was a popular story with country folk many years ago.
   Notes: *The popularity of the story stems from its championing the plight of the poor and the oppressed peasants against the rich, strong, oppressive landlord/ landowner. You can extend this by reading, or encouraging the children to find and read, extracts from 'Robin Hood'.*

3. Has anyone ever tried to cheat you, or someone you know? Write about what happened.
   Notes: *This question is looking for pupils to empathise with feelings surrounding a particular incident.*

2. Think back to one day in your life when something important happened. It might be happy or sad, or exciting or just unusual. Write a log, or diary, for that day, including details of your feelings and emotions.
   Notes: *This question calls for pupils to record their feelings in as much depth as possible.*

Notes: *If you wish to, you can make a teaching point of how the passage shows that language changes over time. The original text, for example, hyphenates 'grind-stone' and 'great-coat' whereas these are now spelled as one word.*

Unit 13 Robinson Crusoe's Log

Do you remember?
selecting correct answers

Pupils should select the correct answer from three possible choices.

1. How did Robinson Crusoe come to be on the island?
   c) Robinson Crusoe was shipwrecked on the island.
2. How long has he been there?
   c) He has been on the island for eight days.
3. What happened to the rest of the crew?
   b) The rest of the crew were drowned.
4. What pleasant surprise did Robinson Crusoe get on the eighth day?
   a) Japp, the captain's dog, came bounding along the beach.
5. Why does he think he will get a good sleep tonight?
   b) He has managed to build a tent.

More to think about
character empathy; making lists from passage

1. What, for Robinson Crusoe, do you think was the most important thing he was recording in his eighth day entry?
   c) Despite all the likely problems ahead he is well satisfied
   with what he has done so far.
2. Why do you think he is feeling pleased with what he has done?
   Notes: *This question calls for pupils to empathise with the fact that Robinson Crusoe has been through a very difficult period, and he is now beginning to realise that he will survive.*
3. List in your book the items he retrieved from the wreck. Which do you think will be most useful? Why?
   tools, a drill, a dozen hatchets, grind-stone, crowbars, nails and rivets, sails, ropes, poles, (gun)powder, musket balls, muskets, shotguns, hammock, mattress, blankets, clothes, great-coats, food.
   Notes: *Evaluating the usefulness of each item is an excellent starting point for other creative activities that will encourage empathy with Robinson Crusoe, including painting and model-making.*

Now try these
facts/feelings; emotional empathy

1. In his log Robinson Crusoe records facts about what he has done, but doesn't tell us much about his thoughts. How do you think he would have been feeling?
   Notes: *The opportunity lends itself to exploring the notion that we might all have different thoughts and feelings about being stranded alone on a desert island. After the children have written their answers to this question, invite selected children to read their responses to the group, and discuss their feelings and the reasons for them.*

Unit 14 I go Chicken-Dippy

Do you remember?
cloze from passage

1. The only thing the chicken had known since she hatched had been other chickens and *wire netting.*
2. Even being stung by fierce little cold *raindrops* felt wonderful.
3. The noise the *wind* made was deafening.
4. Being outside in the fresh *air* was great.
5. But the chicken had never realised how many different *smells* go to make up fresh air.

More to think about
deductive answering in sentences

Pupils should write sentences in their own words to answer each question.

1. Why is the passage called 'I go chicken-dippy'?
   The passage is called 'I go chicken-dippy' to give the sense that the chicken was so overwhelmed with her freedom from the chicken shed that it was almost as though she went slightly mad.
2. Why did the chicken say she couldn't handle it at all?
   She found it difficult to handle all the new sensations, all at once.
3. The author has written mostly in short, sharp sentences. Why do you think this might be?
   The short, sharp sentences convey the impression of a chicken's short, sharp movements.
4. What things do you think the chicken was most pleased to have left behind?
   Pupils may refer to the choking atmosphere at weekends when the chicken shed was not cleaned out.
5. What aspects of her new environment did the chicken find difficult to handle at first?
   The most difficult thing to handle was simply being away from the immediate and close contact with hundreds of other birds, tightly packed together.
6. What message is the author trying to get across to her readers in this passage?
   The author's basic message is that animals have feelings, and suffer if not handled kindly and kept in appropriate conditions.

Now try these
fact/opinion; emotional response; review

Notes: *Each of the questions in this section will be individual to each pupil, but the issues posed are big ones, with various and sometimes conflicting arguments attached to them. For this reason it may be felt that a higher standard of written response from the children will be achieved if the issues have first been considered in discussion with the whole group or class. It is also significant that there is an increasing political awareness of the need for greater compassion in farming, especially with regard to poultry. For this reason, the work* can be extended by encouraging pupils who would like to do so to express their feelings in the form of a letter to their MP or MEP.

1. Chickens are usually kept in huge flocks packed into sheds or in very small cages because farmers can produce eggs and chickens for food much more cheaply that way. Many people wouldn't be able to afford to buy eggs and chicken if they were all allowed to run free in fields. Also, more of the chickens would be killed by foxes if they were running free. How do you think chickens should be kept? Give reasons for your answer.

2. Imagine that you have had a serious accident and have been told you can't leave your bed for many months. What would you miss most? Think especially of some of the very ordinary things we usually take for granted. Make a list, and say why you will miss each thing.

3. This passage is from *The Chicken Gave It to Me* by Anne Fine. Do you feel that you would now like to read the rest of the book? Write a few sentences to explain why.

Now try these
application of knowledge

Notes: As well as being a comprehension activity, this unit has also been devised to teach the use of contents and indexes in information books. For this reason the following activities which extend and apply the concepts are important. You will, no doubt, develop further activities to ensure these fundamental research skills are practised until fully and thoroughly embedded.

1. Find an information book in your classroom or library. Write about how the Contents and Index compare to the ones for *'River'*.
   a) Are they clearer or more complicated?
   b) Do they have more or fewer entries?
   c) Of the two, which Contents and which Index would you prefer to use? Give your reasons.

2. Borrow another information book from your library. Make up some questions using the Contents and Index, like those in this unit. Ask a friend to answer them.

Unit 15 Finding Your Way About

Do you remember?
cloze from passage

1. 'River' is an information book in a series called *Landshapes*.
2. There are *12* books in the series.
3. There is a Contents page at the front of *'River'*.
4. At the back is the *Index* page.
5. The Index tells us *where* to find information.

More to think about
one-word deductive answers

1. Write a number or words to answer each question about the Contents page.
   a) How many main chapters are there in 'River'? *4*
   b) What is the first chapter about? *How rivers work*
   c) On which page does Chapter 1 begin? *10*
   d) What is on pages 2 and 3 in the book? *World map*
   e) What else comes before the first chapter?
      Contents page; Facts about rivers; Introduction
   f) List the names of the other chapters. *Rivers in hills and mountains; Rivers on plains; Rivers of the world*
   g) Into how many sections is Chapter 2 divided? *3*
   h) In which chapter would you find a section about 'What floods do'? *Chapter 3*
   i) How many pages are used to describe the River Nile? *2*
   j) On what page is the Index? *37*

2. Write a number or words to answer each question about the Index.
   a) Which two pages should you turn to for information about the Amazon? *4, 34*
   b) How many pages carry information about pebbles? *5*
   c) To which pages would you turn to find out about floods? *10, 15, 26, 28, 30*
   d) Where could you find out what a 'shoal' is? *page 15*
   e) In which chapter is the page with the reference to Cairo? *Chapter 4*
   f) In which chapter is the page with the reference to water plants? *Chapter 1*
   g) On how many pages can you read about sand? *4*
   h) On how many pages can you read about waterfalls? *3*

Unit 16 Sedna, the Great Inuit Goddess

Do you remember?
true/false/can't tell literal responses

Write in your book 'true', 'false', or 'can't tell' for each one.
1. The Inuits collected most of their food from the sea. *true*
2. Sedna was born to two ordinary Inuits *false*
3. She had two sisters. *can't tell*
4. Sedna grew very quickly. *true*
5. She had an enormous appetite. *true*
6. She even tried to eat her own parents! *true*
7. Her grandmother said she was such a difficult child because her parents hadn't been strict enough. *can't tell*
8. Her parents put her in a boat and hoped they wouldn't see her again. *false*
9. Her parents took her out to sea and threw her overboard. *true*
10. She sank to the bottom of the sea and became the goddess of all the sea creatures. *true*

More to think about
deductive answering in sentences; summarising

1. *Pupils should write a sentence in their own words to answer each question.*
   a) Why might the land of the Inuits be described as 'inhospitable'?
      The icy wastes of the land of the Inuits prevent any vegetation, and so the people can't grow food or find building materials, such as wood and stone.
   b) Do you think the two giants were proud of their baby when she was first born?
      Yes, at first they would have thought she was an ordinary baby.
   c) What went wrong?
      Sedna grew much faster and bigger than even a giant's baby should have grown.
   d) What made them realise they needed to do something drastic?
      Sedna tried to eat her parents.
   e) How do we know that the 'baby' had become very big by the time her parents took her out to sea?
      Sedna's parents were afraid that she might overturn the canoe.
   f) Even though Sedna was a monster, how can we tell that the writer felt rather sorry for her?
      In the last paragraph the writer refers to 'poor Sedna'.

2. Write a summary of the story in your own words. Pick out the main points and use no more than 50 words.

Now try these
vocabulary work; character and setting empathy; review

1. Read this part of the passage again. Copy it neatly into your book but, without changing the meanings, write other words in place of the eight words printed in heavy type.

   Long, long ago, two giants gave birth to a baby girl. But she did not **remain** a small baby for long. She had such an **enormous** appetite and **consumed** so much food that she quickly grew very big indeed. Any joints of meat that she saw she would grab and **gluttonously** gobble up. Keeping the child fed was becoming an **increasingly desperate** task, causing the two old giants terrible **anguish**.

   One night as the giants lay sleeping, they felt great pains in their legs. They awoke, and to their horror and utter **astonishment** realised that Sedna was trying to eat them!

   Notes: *There are several possible alternatives for each of the words. Discuss this in groups, comparing different children's suggestions. This is a good opportunity to introduce the children to the use of a thesaurus, subsequent use of which can be part of a class weekly 'drill', together with regular dictionary and spelling activities. Pupils can find this enjoyable as well as highly productive as a routine. But, ultimately, the point of the regular exercises is to give pupils the confidence to refer frequently to both a thesaurus and a dictionary whenever appropriate during normal writing activities.*

2. The action of the two giants was a dramatic one. Describe how you think they must have felt on their outward journey, and then on their return homeward.
   Notes: *This question looks for pupils to empathise with characters in a certain setting and situation.*

3. To this day Inuits live in the inhospitable white wilderness of the Arctic wastes of Northern Canada. Describe how you think life would be, its problems and its pleasures. If you can, find a reference book to help you before you start; if not, just use your imagination.
   Notes: *Again, this question looks for pupils to use empathy to 'think themselves into' a certain setting and situation, and explore their feelings.*

4. How did this story leave you feeling? Write a letter to your friend explaining your reactions, and whether you think he or she should now read it.
   Notes: *This activity gives a convenient, structured opportunity to revise the formal aspects of laying out a letter. It calls for pupils to review the text and gives them a reason for writing persuasively about their judgement of it.*

Unit 17 From a Railway Carriage

Do you remember?
literal answering in sentences

Pupils should write a sentence in their own words to answer each question.

1. What animals are in the meadow as the train passes?
   Horses and cattle are in the meadow as the train passes.
2. What has been recently painted?
   Some of the stations have recently been painted.
3. What is the child collecting?
   The child is gathering brambles.

4. Who stands and watches the train pass by?
   A tramp watches the train.
5. What is near to the river?
   A mill is close to the river.

More to think about
deductive answering in sentences

Pupils should write sentences in their own words to answer each question.

1. What clues can you find in the poem that shows it was written many years ago?
   We wouldn't see a loaded runaway cart now. The poem also refers to a mill, although some old mills are still standing today.
2. How does the poet describe the speed of the train?
   'Faster than fairies, faster than witches', and 'charging along like troops in a battle'.
3. What phrases does he use to tell that a large number of sights fly past very quickly?
   The poet says that the sights 'fly as thick as driving rain'.
4. How does the way the poet has written this famous poem make you think of a train rushing along a track?
   The rhythm of the poem sounds like a train hurtling along over a railway track.
   Notes: *Poems with strong rhythms can be great fun when used for choral speaking (groups reading the poem together as a small choir might sing). Another well-known poem about railways, which also has a strong beat, is Royal Mail, although unfortunately modern welded tracks don't have the same strong, rhythmic beat as the old lines! This could be a useful discussion point.*

Now try these
matching rhyming words; review; empathy with incidents

1. Write down these words and then find a word in the poem that rhymes with each of them.
   a) witches *ditches* b) cattle *battle* c) rain *plain*
   d) eye *by* e) scrambles *brambles* f) gazes *daisies*
   g) road *load*
2. Now write two extra rhyming words of your own to go with the pairs you have just written.
3. Did you enjoy this poem? What is it about the poem that you liked most? Give your reasons.
   Notes: *This question requires pupils to review the poem, giving persuasive reasons for their judgements about it.*
4. Going on any long journey is exciting. Write about a journey you have been on, and say how you felt, both before you went and while you were travelling.
   Notes: *This question calls for pupils to empathise with feelings surrounding a particular incident.*

Unit 18 The Snow Spider

Do you remember?
cloze from passage

1. After tea Mr Griffiths went to his *workshop*.
2. Gwyn left his mother talking to the *cat*.
3. When he reached his *bedroom* he found the door open.
4. There were *shadows* on the wall.
5. The spider was *glowing* in the dark.
6. It felt *cold* when he touched it.
7. He held the spider for several *minutes*.
8. He sat on his *bed* and read his book.

More to think about
deductive answering in sentences; establishing character traits

1. Pupils should write a sentence in their own words to answer each question.
   a) What made Gwyn think his father wanted to avoid conversation?
      Gwyn's father always seemed to have more and more work that he needed to do in his workshop.
   b) What does the author mean when she says Gwyn did not want to show 'an unnatural enthusiasm for bed'?
      Gwyn didn't normally like to go to bed early, so he didn't want to raise suspicions by now seeming as though he wanted to go to bed before his normal bedtime.
   c) When Gwyn reached his room he saw the shadows of seven helmeted figures. What was his reaction?
      Gwyn was scared by the shadows – he froze.
   d) What were they really?
      The shadows were being made by his toy spacemen, standing on the chest of drawers.
   e) What, apart from its glow, was unusual about Gwyn's spider?
      The spider was icy cold.
   f) What does 'it was an exceptional sensation' mean?
      The phrase means 'a very unusual and strange feeling'.
2. Write a short word picture of each of the three characters in the passage: Gwyn, Mr Griffiths and Mrs Griffiths. Think especially about the clues you get about their personalities from the passage. What can you tell about the relationship between Gwyn and his father?
   Notes: *As this question is looking for quite subtle answers about how the characters relate to one another, it would probably be helpful for most children if the work is introduced through group or class discussion.*

Now try these
vocabulary/dictionary work; outcome prediction; emotional response

1. Use a dictionary to help you to match each of these definitions to a word in the grid.
   The first one has been done for pupils, as an example.
   a) get smaller *C1*   b) disappear *A1*
   c) extremely beautiful *B2*   d) get bigger *B1*
   e) not moving *A2*   f) completely changed *A3*
   g) feeling *C3*   h) exceptional *B3*   i) not very deep *C2*
2. What do you think happened in the end? Make notes of how you think the story might finish.
   Notes: *This question requires pupils to deduce from what has gone before what a predictable outcome might be.*
3. Although Gwyn wasn't frightened of spiders, many people are. Others are scared by different small creatures, like mice or rats or snakes. You might be worried by something quite different, like thunder-storms, or the dark. Say what frightens you the most, and try to explain why, and describe how you feel when you are frightened.
   Notes: *Initially some children will feel reluctant to divulge such personal anxieties, and some never will. But for some children, being given the opportunity to express their fears, and to share them with others, can be helpful. The teacher 'confessing' to some small phobia can often get a discussion started. The work can be usefully extended into other creative forms, both written, such as poetry, and illustrative.*

Unit 19 Ginger

Do you remember?
selecting correct answer

Pupils should select the correct answer from two possible choices given.
1. Which horse is describing its early life?
   a) Ginger is describing her early life.
2. When was Ginger taken from her mother?
   b) She was taken from her mother as soon as she was weaned.
3. Did she get on well with the other young horses?
   a) Yes, Ginger was pleased to be with the other colts.
4. Why didn't she like the boys who came through her field?
   a) The boys threw stones at the horses.
5. Was Ginger's breaking-in a good time for her?
   a) No, the men were cruel to her.

More to think about
deductive answering in sentences

Pupils should write a sentence in their own words to answer each question.
1. Ginger said her master did not ill-use her, but he did not care for her. What does she mean by this?
   Ginger's master wasn't deliberately cruel, but he was thoughtless about how he treated her.
2. Why did she think all boys were her enemy?
   The only boys Ginger had seen had been cruel to her.
3. When, as a young horse, was Ginger most content?
   Ginger was at her happiest when galloping up and down the free meadows with the other young horses.
4. In the third main paragraph she says 'this was the first experience I had of men's kindness'. She was being sarcastic. What does sarcastic mean?
   Being sarcastic is saying the opposite of what you mean, in a sharp or bitter way to show you are cross.
5. Why was the man who was trying to break-in Ginger called Samson?
   He was called Samson because he was big and strong.
6. Why was she so upset that he described her as 'horse-flesh'?
   Ginger felt that Samson calling her 'horse flesh' showed that he didn't see her as a young horse with feelings, but as an animal with no feelings.

Now try these
vocabulary work; correcting sentences; character empathy and imaginative description

1. Find these phrases again. They all come from the last paragraph. Copy them, and next to each say what it means.
   a) put him out of temper   *made him annoyed*
   b) he chucked me hard   *he tugged me roughly*
   c) my blood was thoroughly up   *I felt very cross and absolutely determined*
   d) I cared for nothing he could do   *I didn't care whatever he did*
   e) my persecutor   *the person being cruel and unkind to me*
2. One word in each sentence is wrong. Can you spot the mistakes? Write each sentence correctly in your book.
   a) *Ginger <u>was</u> pleased not to be with her old master.*
   b) *Ginger and Black Beauty <u>were</u> friends.*
   c) *The boys passing <u>through</u> the field threw stones.*
   d) *Ginger <u>ran</u> around in the meadow with the other colts.*
   e) *She galloped <u>off</u> to the end of the field.*

3. Except in stories like this, animals can't speak, but like us they can feel pain. They also learn to have feelings about people, so they can think. Imagine that you are an animal that you know. Write about your life and feelings. Tell your readers about: where you are kept; what you are fed; whether you have other animal friends; how your owners treat you; anything you really wish could be changed.
Notes: *This question requires pupils to use empathy to 'think themselves into' the animal's situation and explore that animal's feelings, also writing in an imaginative way about the animal they have chosen to be. Black Beauty lends itself to a wealth of language work, and can be developed into a theme which can carry not just comprehension but English work across the particular curriculum being followed. And it should not be overlooked that Black Beauty is an excellent book to read aloud.*

Unit 20 Horses of the Sun

Do you remember?
cloze from passage

1. *Phaeton* was the son of Helios.
2. Helios was the Greek *sun* god.
3. Phaeton wanted to be allowed to drive his father's *chariot.*
4. Helios warned him not to guide the *horses.*
5. Phaeton took the chariot too close to his *village.*
6. Zeus, the father of the gods, sent a *thunderbolt* to stop the disaster.

More to think about
summary; sequencing; deductive answering in sentences

1. Write a summary of the events that led to Phaeton's death. Try not to use more than 60 words.
2. Here are some of the events from the story. Copy them into your book in the right order.
   Phaeton begged his father, Helios, to be allowed to drive the chariot across the sky.
   Helios agreed, on condition that his son allowed the horses freedom to take their own route.
   Phaeton saw his village, and wanted everyone to see him.
   The stallions hurtled downwards.
   The flames and heat severely damaged the Earth.
   Zeus sent a thunderbolt that threw Phaeton out of the chariot.
   Phaeton was killed.
   Zeus changed Phaeton's body into a cool stream.
3. *Pupils should write a sentence in their own words to answer each question.*
   a) What was Phaeton's main reason for wanting to drive his father's chariot?
      Phaeton wanted to show off to the people in his village.
   b) What was the chariot really? What clues make you think this?
      The chariot was the sun. The story tells us that it was called the sun chariot. It follows an arc across the sky towards the west. When it started its journey, light began to climb into the dark sky. When it came too close to the earth its heat burnt the crops and buildings and dried up the rivers.
   c) Why were the ancient people of Greece more likely to have legends about the sun than early people in countries like Britain?
      For much of the year the sun shines from cloudless skies in Greece, whereas in Britain it is more often cloudy so we are less aware of the sun.

d) When Phaeton was over his village he said, 'No one will see that it is me driving the chariot.' What does this tell you about him?
   Phaeton was rather a show off. He wanted people to think he was clever and important.

Now try these
examining figurative language; forming opinions; incident empathy

1. The authors have used some interestingly descriptive phrases. Find in the passage, and copy into your book, how they describe:
   a) the first light of dawn   *Light began to climb into the dark sky and the restless horses leaped into the waiting blackness.*
   b) what happened to Phaeton after he was hit by the thunderbolt   *its power sent him spinning out of the chariot. His body twisted in space until it landed, broken, on the Earth.*
   c) Phaeton's sisters' tears   *pieces of golden amber, glinting in the sunlight.*
   d) the poplar trees   *slender poplar trees which swayed and whispered sorrowfully in the wind.*

2. Many myths and legends like this one have a hidden moral, or meaning. What is the moral of this story?
   It is wise to listen to others who may know better than you, and think carefully before being tempted to show off to your friends.

3. Adults often ask young people not to do things that may be dangerous or cause problems. Write about something you have done, that you had been asked not to, or knew you shouldn't, or wish that you hadn't!
   Notes: *This question calls for pupils to use empathy to 'think themselves into' a particular situation and explore their feelings.*

Progress Unit B

Do you remember?
literal answering in sentences

Score: 2 marks for each correct answer (maximum 10 marks).

Pupils should write a sentence in their own words to answer each question.

1. Who were cleaning up the park?
   The park was being cleaned by anglers, conservation volunteers, Cubs and Brownies.
2. What was the event called?
   It was the RESCUE event.
3. Was there more or less rubbish this year than last?
   There was less rubbish this year than last year.
4. What was found recently in a litter bin?
   A large amount of engine oil was found in a litter bin.
5. Who was pleased to see so many young people helping?
   The town's mayor, Mr Jack Alaman, was pleased that the young people were helping.

More to think about
deductive answering in sentences; selecting true statements

Score: Q1 1 mark for each correct answer and deduct 1 mark for each incorrect answer; Q2 2 marks for a correct answer to each section (maximum 13 marks).

1. Read these sentences about the newspaper report. Neatly copy only the ones that are true into your book.
   The Cubs and Brownies helped the anglers and conservation volunteers.

Some people were cleaning up the river while others worked in the park.
This year there was much less rubbish than three years ago.
Some people drop their garden litter in the park rather than taking it to the refuse dump.
The mayor, Mr Alaman, was pleased with the clean-up.

2. *Pupils should write a sentence in their own words to answer each question.*
   a) Why were so many people prepared to give up their free time to clean up other people's litter?
   Most people like to live in a clean and pleasant environment, and many are prepared to help to make it that way.
   b) What do you think is the advantage of having one big RESCUE event each year rather than a few people going out each weekend?
   It is easier to get a lot of people enthusiastic if they feel they are part of one big event.
   c) Can you think of reasons why the amount of litter has been going down each year?
   Possible answers might include:
   a) *we are all becoming more conscious of our environment*
   b) *the publicity for the annual RESCUE event has made people more aware of the need to take their litter home.*
   d) What does the mayor mean when he says, 'But you always get a few who spoil it for the many'?
   There will always be a few people who don't care, and their litter will make the park and other open spaces untidy for the majority of people who do take the trouble not to leave litter lying about.

Now try these
establishing arguments; promoting opinions
Score: the marks awarded in this section are discretionary, according to your judgement. The pieces need not be awarded marks individually; what is significant is the extent to which pupils are beginning to establish reasonable arguments and promote opinions. For this reason an alternative to asking for all the questions to be completed is for pupils to be allowed to select just one or two tasks, and for these to be worked on in more depth. Marks towards the higher end of the scale should be reserved for those presenting their work in well constructed, and appropriately punctuated sentences (maximum 7 marks).

1. Huge amounts of money are spent on putting things into packages. These boxes, wrappings and so on, create an enormous amount of rubbish. Write a sentence to answer each of these questions.
   a) Why do manufacturers put so many items in expensive packaging?
   Possible answers include:
   i) *to attract the customer's attention*
   ii) *to make their product look better than a competitor's*
   iii) *to make it look worth more*
   iv) *to protect the product from damage*
   b) Who pays for the packaging in the end?
   The cost of the packaging is part of the total cost of the product, so in the end the customer pays for the packaging.
   c) Easter Eggs have expensive packaging, and so do many toys. How would you feel if you were given presents that didn't have colourful boxes?
   d) What would be the disadvantages if supermarkets sold items like sugar, or butter, or eggs without packaging?
   Possible answers include problems with:
   i) *damage to delicate products, such as eggs*
   ii) *expense of having staff to weigh out loose products, such as sugar*
   iii) *higher level of wastage*
   iv *possible reduction in cleanliness*
   v) *Which items that you use at home could be sold without packaging?*
2. How would you solve the problem of people dropping litter? Describe how you would run a publicity campaign, and draw a small version of a poster for it. Think carefully about the wording to go on your poster.
3 Write a letter to your Member of Parliament saying what sort of punishments you suggest for people who continued to dump their rubbish and waste in public places. Explain your reasons.

Indicative scores for National Curriculum

Below level 3	Level 3	Level 4	Level 5
0-9	10-23	24-27	28-30

Indicative scores for 5–14 Guidelines

Level A	Level B	Level C	Level D
0-4	5-16	17-27	28-30

Book 4

Scope and sequence of skills

Unit	Title	Page	Do you remember? *Reading the lines*	More to think about *Reading between the lines*	Now try these *Reading beyond the lines*
1	**Trouble Half-Way** *Modern fiction*	4	cloze from passage	literal and inferential answering in sentences	figurative language; empathy
2	**Crack-a-Dawn** *Modern poem*	7	selecting the correct answer	deduction; summary	empathy; outcome prediction
3	**The Trojan War** *Myths and legends*	10	true/false/can't tell	inference and deduction; empathy	vocabulary enrichment; deduction
4	**The Discontented Fish** *Texts from other cultures*	14	literal answering in sentences	inference; summary	figurative language; empathy; evaluation
5	**Different Views of Winter** *Modern poems*	18	cloze	literal; deduction	review; empathy
6	**Shen Nung** *Texts from other cultures*	20	cloze from passage	inference; deduction	vocabulary enrichment; evaluation
7	**Colonel Fazackerley** *Modern poem*	22	literal answering in sentences	sequencing; inference	empathy; deduction
8	**Advertisements** *Comparing advertisements*	24	literal answering in sentences	evaluation	evaluation; appreciative responses
9	**The Railway Children** *Long-established fiction*	26	selecting the correct answer	inference; summarising	figurative language; evaluation

Unit	Title	Page	Do you remember? *Reading the lines*	More to think about *Reading between the lines*	Now try these *Reading beyond the lines*
10	**Gulliver's Travels** *Long-established fiction*	29	true/false/can't tell; literal answering in sentences	deductive answering in sentences; character empathy	vocabulary enrichment; summary; situation empathy
	Progress Unit A *Fable*	32	cloze	sequencing; deduction	review; character empathy
11	**A Smugglers' Song** *Classic poem*	35	selecting the correct answers	deductive answering in sentences	listing; deduction; empathy
12	**The BFG** *Modern fiction*	38	literal answering in sentences	inference; deduction	vocabulary development; empathy; appreciation
13	**The King, Compere Lapin and Compere Tig** *Tales from other cultures*	42	matching questions and answers	literal answering in sentences	evaluation; empathy; outcome prediction
14	**Looking Down** *Aerial photograph*	44	sentence completion	deductive answering in sentences	vocabulary enrichment
15	**Save It!** *Newspaper report*	46	selecting the correct answer	summary; literal; deduction	establishing arguments
16	**The Phantom Tollbooth** *Myth from other cultures*	48	cloze	literal and deductive answering in sentences	empathy
17	**The TV Kid** *Modern fiction*	51	true/false/can't tell	summary; deduction; outcome prediction	empathy
18	**Hiawatha's Childhood** *Classic poem*	54	cloze from passage	deductive answering in sentences	use of rhythm; empathy
19	**Martin's Mice** *Modern fiction*	57	literal answering in sentences	inference and deduction; figurative language	evaluation; prediction
20	**Deserts** *Map, diagram, information text*	60	literal	deductive answering in sentences	vocabulary enrichment; note-making; empathy
	Progress Unit B *Tales from other cultures*	63	literal answering in sentences	deductive answering in sentences; summary	evaluation; vocabulary enrichment

Unit 1 Trouble Half-Way

Do you remember?
cloze from passage
1. Amy's mother's new husband was *Mr Ermins (Richard)*.
2. Her father had *died*.
3. Amy's mother was doing the *ironing*.
4. *Miss Oxley* was Amy's teacher.
5. Debra hurt her *ankle* on the beam.
6. Mother asked Richard if he stood on one leg in *assembly*.

More to think about
literal and inferential answering in sentences
1. Pupils should write a sentence in their own words to answer each question.
   a) What relation was Helen to Amy?
   Helen was Amy's sister.
   b) Why did Amy need to get used to Mr Ermins?
   Mr Ermins was her new stepfather.

c) Why didn't her mother want Amy to call Mr Ermins Richard?
Amy's mother said Amy wouldn't have called her father by his first name.
d) Why did Richard think it was unnecessary to iron nappies?
Richard said Helen wouldn't know whether her napkins were ironed or not.
e) Why didn't Amy want to make a fuss about her bad knee?
She wanted to be able to practise for the competition on Thursday.
2. What clues are there in the passage that show Richard and Amy's mother were feeling rather irritated with each other?
Richard was criticising the way Mother was ironing, and Mother was getting cross that he was being critical of her and what Amy did in the school assembly.

Now try these
figurative language; empathy

1. Find these phrases in the passage. Write them in different words the author could have used without changing the meaning.
   a) Mum would retort   *Mum would answer/say/reply*
   b) the tottering pile   *the wobbly/unsteady pile*
   c) Life's too short.   *There are more important things to worry about.*
   d) The socks were gyving round her ankles
      The socks had slipped and were crumpled/wrinkled around her ankles

2. Imagine that you are Amy. Write a letter to a friend describing Richard, your feelings about him, and how you get on with him.

3. What do *you* think Amy should have called Richard? Give your reasons.

4. As for Amy and Helen, it is always terribly sad if a parent dies. It is also very difficult for children if their parents separate. Apart from the unhappiness of not having both parents together, make two lists of the problems you could imagine when a mother or father brings a new partner to live with the family.
   Pupils are asked to make their lists under the headings: 'Problems for the children', and 'Problems for the new partner'.

Notes: *Questions 2,3 and 4 have been devised to encourage empathy with the central child character in the passage, and in particular to explore her family relationships. For some children this will be particularly pertinent, and for many the process of exorcising some of their own pain and hurt through a fictional character can be helpful, but obviously you will need to exercise care and sensitivity. One or more of the questions might initially be discussed with the class or a group, with you tabulating the main points suggested.*

Unit 2 Crack-a-Dawn

Do you remember?
selecting the correct answer

Pupils are asked to select the correct answer to each question from two possible choices.

1. What was the boy's name?
   a) The boy's name was Darren.
2. What did his mother give him for breakfast?
   a) His mother took him crack-a-dawn cereal for breakfast.
3. Where did she take Darren's breakfast?
   a) She took it to him in bed.
4. What was the weather like?
   b) The weather outside was fine.
5. If he misses the bus, how is Darren to get to school?
   b) Darren will need to go to school by taxi.
6. Whose name did Darren misspell?
   a) Darren spelled his dad's name wrong.
7. Why was his mother cross?
   a) She was cross because he had missed his bus on the last two mornings.

More to think about
deduction; summary

1. *Pupils should write a sentence in their own words to answer each question.*
   a) Why do you think the poem is called Crack-a-Dawn?
      The poem is named after the cereal Darren eats.

   b) What does Darren's mother mean by 'the weather outside is fine – at least by North Sea standards'?
      Darren's mother is pretending that the weather is good when really it is bad.
   c) Has the gerbil really been eaten by the dog? Why does Mum say it has?
      The dog hasn't eaten the gerbil, but Darren's mother says it has in order to shock Darren into getting up quickly.
   d) What is Darren's favourite sport?
      Darren's favourite sport is soccer/football.

2. Write a word picture of Darren's mum. Think carefully about the words you might use to describe her from the clues in the poem.
   Notes: *It can sometimes be useful to extend a piece of descriptive deduction work of this sort by developing it into a comparison between the character and another 'real' person, such as in this case the pupil's own mother.*

3. What is the main idea of the poem? Write a brief summary of what happens, using no more than 30 words.
   Notes: *This calls for pupils to both deduce what the poem is 'about' and summarise this point effectively.*

Now try these
empathy; outcome prediction

1. We all have some habits which other people find annoying or irritating. Write about some of the things that you do that make your friends or family cross.
   Notes: *This question calls for pupils to show empathy towards friends/members of their family.*

2. Make a list of some of the things that other people in your home do that make you cross. Say why these things irritate you.
   Notes: *This question calls for pupils to use empathy to 'think themselves into' this situation, and to explore their feelings.*

3. What do you think happened in the end? Write four more lines for the poem.
   Notes: *This question calls for pupils to think back over the poem, and deduce from what has happened/what the poem is 'about' what a predictable outcome might be. Pupils should engage with the poem and use their imaginations to construct an ending.*

4. Write a nonsense verse.
   Pupils are given a format/example,
   'If I were to lay all day in bed
   My dad would pour water on my head.
   If I were to...'

Unit 3 The Trojan War

Do you remember?
true/false/can't tell

Read these sentences about the Trojan War. Write in your book 'true', 'false', or 'can't tell' for each one.

1. The Trojan War was fought between the people of Troy and Greece.   *true*
2. Most of the Greek soldiers came from the city of Athens.   *can't tell*
3. Menelaus was the king of Greece.   *true*
4. His wife was Helen.   *true*
5. Paris forced Helen to run away with him.   *false*
6. They eloped while Menelaus was visiting his mother.   *can't tell*
7. Achilles was the greatest hero Greek has ever had.   *false*

8. It was totally impossible for him to be killed.   *false*
9. The Greeks built the Trojan Horse.   *true*
10. The Greeks won the Trojan War, and Helen returned to Greece.   *true*

More to think about
inference and deduction; empathy

1. In your own words, describe what caused the Greeks to declare war on the Trojans.
   The main cause of the war was the refusal of the Trojans to send Helen back to Greece.
2. Why do you think Helen didn't go away with Paris as soon as he asked her?
   Helen was already married to Menelaus, and she thought it would be wrong to leave him.
3. What clues can you find in the passage to show that the two armies were fairly evenly matched?
   Although the brave soldiers on both sides continued to fight and to die, neither side seemed able to get the upper hand. It was only when the Greeks devised a trick that they eventually overcame theTrojans.
4. Imagine that you are Odysseus. Write a letter to King Menelaus describing in detail your plan for winning the war, and explaining why you're sure it will work.
   Notes: *This question calls for pupils to use empathy to 'think themselves into' Odysseus's character and situation.*

Now try these
vocabulary enrichment; deduction

1. Use a dictionary to help you to match each of these definitions to a word in the grid.
   The first one has been done for pupils, as an example.
   a) reveal, or let out *C1*   b) at once, or immediately *B3*
   c) in the end *A1*   d) invent, or worked out *A3*
   e) lift with effort *B1*   f) impossible to beat *C3*
   g) fascinated *C2*   h) at first *B2*   i) make sure *A2*
2. What do the following phrases mean? Write them in your own words.
   a) they secretly eloped
      the two lovers ran away together
   b) the king's bewilderment and anger
      the king's surprise and extreme annoyance
   c) hitherto invincible hero
      the previously unbeatable warrior
   d) unbeknown to the Trojans
      the Trojans did not realise
   e) It was a rout!
      It was an easy and complete victory.
3. The Trojan War occurred thousands of years ago. Which parts of the passage do you think are basically true, and which parts have become altered over the years?
   Notes: *This activity provides a useful opportunity to consider with the whole class the way that stories become modified and sometimes exaggerated with retelling. Play a game of Chinese whispers to prove the point. Consider other stories which might have been modified over the years.*

Unit 4 The Discontented Fish

Do you remember?
literal answering in sentences

Pupils should write a sentence in their own words to answer each question.
1. Where did the big fish live?
   The big fish lived in a small pool.
2. Who else lived with him in the pool?
   A colony of little fish also lived in the pool.
3. Why did the big fish want to leave the pool?
   He was disturbed and irritated by the smaller fish.
4. When was he able to leave the pool?
   He was able to leave the pool when the river flooded.
5. What happened when he first reached the river?
   He found that there were fish bigger than him who were determined to bully him, and eventually to eat him.
6. Who bit him in the tail?
   He was bitten in the tail by a large tiger-fish.
7. Did he stay in the river?
   No, he decided to return to the river.
8. If so, why? If not, why not?
   He thought that he would be safer and happier in the pool.

More to think about
inference; summary

1. Pupils should write a sentence in their own words to answer each question.
   a) Why does the author describe the pool as 'a happy pool'?
      All, except the big fish, were happy in the pool.
   b) If it was a happy pool, why did the big fish want to leave?
      The big fish was rather isolated from the other, smaller fish, and he thought life would be more to his liking in a bigger environment.
   c) How did the older fish in the pool encourage the big fish to leave?
      The older fish, who were keen to encourage the miserable bigger fish to move on, paid him false compliments saying how clever he was to think of moving on.
   d) Why did the big fish think, 'They obviously didn't realise who I was' when the fish in the river attacked him?
      He thought everyone else thought he was as important as he considered himself to be.
   e) Why, after he returned to the pool, did the big fish not complain about the small fish when they played and splashed?
      The big fish realised that the pool was the best place to be, and he would prefer the mild irritations of the small fish rather than the aggression of the bigger fish in the river.
2. Pupils are given groups of words under three columns headed: 'Who?', 'Does what?', 'When?'. They are asked to take a group of words out of each column to make a sensible sentence. Their sentences should be:
   The big fish escaped into the river when it flooded.
   Some bigger fish drove the big fish away when he was resting.
   Two black and white fish tried to eat the big fish when he was in the crevice.
   The little fishes persuaded the big fish to leave when he was always complaining.
3. Write a brief version of the story using only five sentences.
   Notes: *This question calls for pupils to express the main points as concisely as possible.*

Now try these
figurative language; empathy; evaluation

1. All of these phrases are in the story. What do they mean?
   a) kept himself to himself   *didn't mix with others*
   b) please stop the commotion   *please don't make a noise*
   c) the big fish's constant gripes   *the big fish's non-stop complaining*
   d) their fearful jaws   *their frightening teeth*
   e) he gingerly swam out   *he timidly and carefully emerged*
   f) to effect his escape   *to get away*
2. Have you ever met a person like the big fish? In what ways does the big fish remind you of them?
   Notes: *This question asks pupils to understand the main character, identify its characteristics correctly and show this by applying them appropriately to another character.*
3. This story contains a moral (or message) for humans. Write what you think it is.
   Notes: *This is a useful discussion point, and children can consider examples from their own experiences of when they anticipated that other people's fate was better than their own, although in fact it may well have been worse.*

Unit 5 Different Views of Winter

Do you remember?
cloze

Pupils should note that the following words are missing:
1. *Ogden Nash*   2. *Emma Barnes*   3. *winter*   4. *likes*
5. *hell*   6. *houses*   7. *smooth*   8. *clean*   9. *slushy/going*
10. *scratch*   11. *alone*   12. *play/yell*

More to think about
literal; deduction

1. Make a list of the reasons why Ogden Nash enjoys winter.
   Ogden Nash enjoys watching the shapes made by the snow and imagining what they remind him of, as well as the fun of snow, when he catches it on his tongue.
2. Make a list of the reasons why Emma Barnes dislikes winter.
   Emma Barnes dislikes the ice scratching her hands, her fingers becoming stiff and numb, the problem she has moving her wheelchair about in the snow, and the loneliness when all the other children are off enjoying themselves.
3. Explain in your own words what is meant in 'Winter Morning' by:
   a) Winter is the king of showmen
      In winter the weather does interesting and attractive things to the countryside, especially when it snows or is frosty.
   b) The world looks good enough to bite.
      When the fresh white snow covers everything it looks like a cake that has been iced.
   c) That's the season to be young
      It's good to be young in winter and able to enjoy the snow.
4. Explain in your own words what is meant in 'Winter in a Wheelchair' by:
   a) Icy tyres scratch my hands
      The ice that collects on the tyres of the wheelchair scratches my hands as I push on the wheels to move it.
   b) My independence melts away
      I can't get about in the snow without help.

   c) This winter wonderland of snow
      For me is winter hell.
      While winter is fun for most people, for me it is a miserable time.

Now try these
review; empathy

1. Which of the poems did you prefer? Give your reasons.
   Notes: *The question calls for pupils to review the two poems, writing persuasively about the judgement they make.*
2. Imagine that you are the child in Emma's poem.
   a) Make a list of other things that most children enjoy but, for you in a wheelchair, are difficult or impossible to join in.
   b) Write a letter to your grandmother about when you were invited to go out for a day with a friend's family, and what happened when part of the day was spent at a huge funfair. Write about your feelings, as well as what you did.
   Notes: *While this unit focuses on the problems of a child in a wheelchair, the work might usefully be extended in various ways to consider the problems and difficulties of children with other disabilities having to cope with everyday situations. You can discuss the causes of the problems, such as lack of ramps/easy access, and what can and should be done to help people in these situations. This will be most helpfully explored if there are any children in the class who have a particular disability, but you will need to use your judgement to ensure discussions are sensitively handled.*

Unit 6 Shen Nung

Do you remember?
cloze from passage

1. *Shen Nung* was one of China's greatest *emperors*.
2. Some say he had the *head* of an ox and the body of a *man*.
3. He taught his people how to cultivate *crops* and tame the *forest*.
4. He also showed them how *plants/medicine* could heal them when they were *sick*.
5. Shen Nung boiled some *leaves* and made *tea*.
6. His *wife* mastered the art of breeding *silkworms*.

More to think about
inference; deduction

1. Read these sentences, and write 'true', 'false' or 'can't tell' for each one.
   a) China has only ever had ten emperors.   *false*
   b) Shen Nung was by far the greatest emperor China has ever had.   *false/can't tell*
   c) All early Chinese emperors were thought to be part animal and part human.   *can't tell*
   d) Shen Nung was said to have the head of a man and the body of an ox.   *true*
   e) According to some stories, he was able to invent the plough because he was part ox.   *true*
   f) According to some stories, Shen Nung had a see-through stomach.   *true*
   g) Shen Nung liked tea.   *can't tell*
   h) The leaves of ginseng are thought to clean the blood.   *true*
   i) Ginseng was also soon recognised as a tonic.   *true*
   j) The emperor died when he ate a strange form of grass.   *true*

2. Make a list of Shen Nung's achievements, and those of his wife.
   Shen Nung: invented: the plough; cultivation of crops; taming forests/clearing overgrown woodlands; medical advances. He discovered: tea; discovered ginseng. Shen Nung's wife began: breeding silkworms. She developed house crafts.

Now try these
vocabulary enrichment; evaluation

1. Use a dictionary to find the meaning of each of these words:
   a) successive *following one after another*
   b) productive *producing much*   c) enrich *make richer*
   d) renown *famous*   e) deity *a god or goddess*
   f) primitive *early, ancient*
2. Which parts of this legend do you judge to be basically true, and which parts are probably fictional?
   Notes: *This question calls for pupils to consider and evaluate the legend, based on knowledge and experience they bring from outside the text.*
3. Of Shen Nung's various achievements, which do you judge to be the most important? Give your reasons.
   Notes: *Again, this question requires pupils to make a value judgement based on the evidence. The reasons they give for their answers will be important.*
Notes: *You can extend this unit by applying similar questions and activities to other early rulers of China or other civilisations. This will also give pupils opportunities to practise their research skills.*

Unit 7 Colonel Fazackerley

Do you remember?
literal answers in sentences

Pupils should write a sentence in their own words to answer each question.
1. What was the Colonel's full name?
   The Colonel's full name was Fazackerley Butterworth-Toast.
2. What did he buy?
   He bought an old castle.
3. What did he unexpectedly get with his purchase?
   The castle had a ghost.
4. When and from where did the ghost first appear?
   He saw the ghost on his first evening when it appeared from the chimney.
5. What was the Colonel doing when he saw the ghost?
   He was waiting to dine.

More to think about
sequencing; inference

1. These six sentences about Colonel Fazackerley and the ghost have been muddled up. Write them in the correct order.
   Colonel Fazackerley bought the castle.
   A ghost appeared from the chimney.
   The Colonel joked with the ghost, saying he thought it was going to a Fancy Dress Ball.
   The ghost became increasingly furious.
   The Colonel thought this was really funny.
   The ghost left, and has not been seen since.
2. Was Colonel Fazackerley frightened of the ghost? What makes you think this?
   The colonel wasn't frightened of the ghost. However cross

the ghost became, the colonel was still able to joke with it, pretending he thought it was someone dressed up for a Fancy Dress Ball.
3. Was the ghost pleased Colonel Fazackerley had bought the castle? What did he do to show his feelings?
   The ghost seemed cross, rushing about, making noises, vanishing and reappearing, apparently to frighten off the Colonel.
4. Did the Colonel really want the ghost to stay in the castle? Give the reasons for your answer.
   Notes: *You can encourage some discussion of the last two lines of the poem. (See also Question 3 below.)*

Now try these
empathy; deduction

1. What would you have done if you had met the ghost?
   Notes: *This question calls for pupils to use empathy to 'think themselves into' this situation, and explore their feelings.*
2. What sort of person do you think Colonel Fazackerley was? Use phrases from the poem to help you answer this question.
   Notes: *This question calls for pupils to deduce from clues in the poem what Colonel Fazackerly was like and also to use empathy to help them to understand his character.*
3. What does the poet mean when he says at the end of the poem: 'And then with a smile that was hard to define, Colonel Fazackerley went in to dine'?
   It is possible to deduce from the last lines that the Colonel knew all along that the ghost was real, but that he thought if he pretended it was someone dressed up the ghost would get so cross it would leave.

Unit 8 Advertisements

Do you remember?
literal answering in sentences

Pupils should write a sentence in their own words to answer each question.
1. What are Strobers?
   Strobers are trainers/shoes.
2. How much would a pair of Strobers cost you?
   A pair of Strobers would cost £39.99.
3. Where can you buy them?
   Strobers can be bought in all major department stores and good sports shops.
4. What are the soles made of?
   The soles are made from rubber.
5. Who is promoting the shoes?
   James from Trigger is promoting the shoes.
6. What extra gift do you get if you buy a pair this month?
   If you buy a pair this month you get a free poster.
7. How long is the special offer price available?
   The special offer is available until the end of the month.

More to think about
evaluation

1. There are two advertisements for Strobers.
   a) Which one is more likely to attract your attention? Give your reasons.
      This question calls for pupils to consider and evaluate each advertisement.
   b) What features described are the ones that would most appeal to you?

2. Advertisers want us to feel good about their products.
   a) Which words in the top advertisement are 'feel good' words?
      strong; latest; new; favourite; special; only
   b) Which words are in the advertisement to appeal to sporty people?
      maximum grip; strong tops and laces; seriously sporty
   c) Which words are in the advertisement to appeal to people who want to look cool?
      latest colour range; cool, cute and canny
   d) Which words actually describe the shoes?
      all-rubber soles; strong tops and laces
3. What other devices have been used to persuade you to go out and buy Strobers?
   associating the shoes with a pop star; making them seem less expensive by pricing at £39.99 rather than £40; selling the shoe as a fashion accessory as well as a sports shoe
4. What sort of people do you think the big advertisement is aimed at?
   Would this sort of advertisement encourage you to think about buying Strobers next time you need new trainers?
   Notes: *Pupils should give persuasive reasons for their answers.*

Now try these
evaluation; appreciative responses

1. Why do you think that James, from the new pop group Trigger, has been chosen to be on an advertisement for sports shoes? Do you think well-known personalities do this for nothing, or do they get paid?
2. Give your opinion on these statements:
   a) If you buy something because someone famous has their name on it, it is certain to be good.
   b) If you don't buy immediately when an advertisement with an introductory offer appears, the product is certain to cost more later.
   c) It is sensible for the company to use the word Strobers in this print every time. The brand name is more likely to stick in your mind next time you go to the shops.
   Notes: *These questions look for pupils to make judgements based on knowledge outside the text which they can draw on.*
3. Cut out and stick three advertisements into your book. Write about how well you think each of the advertisements does its job. Give your reasons.
4. Write and design your own advertisement for a new range of mountain bikes. Think of a good brand name, and carefully choose the 'selling' words you are going to use. Finally, make a strong, eye-catching and colourful, visual design.
   Notes: *Advertising in general can be a strong vehicle for helping pupils to appreciate the impact of language on an audience. The model provided in this unit can be repeated with reference to real advertisements as is suggested above. It is worth creating a file of advertisements that particularly lend themselves to these types of exercise through their use of language and interest to young people.*

Unit 9 The Railway Children

Do you remember?
selecting the correct answer
Pupils should select the correct ending from three possible choices.
1. The maid's name was *Ruth.*
2. In the family there were *three children.*
3. Mother said father had to go away *on business.*
4. Next day Mother went to *London.*
5. She arrived home at *seven o'clock.*

More to think about
inference; summary

1. *Pupils should write a sentence in their own words to answer each question.*
   a) What clues can you find to suggest that the family was rich?
      The family had a maid, and the house was large enough to have a library, and they travelled in cabs.
   b) How do you know the story happened nearly 100 years ago?
      Although they were rich they didn't have electricity for lighting; they used gas.
      Notes: *If you wish to, you can make a teaching point of the fact that language changes over time, pointing out that 'armchair' and 'walking shoes' are both hyphenated in the original text.*
   c) How well did Roberta and Peter usually get on with each other?
      Roberta and Peter were inclined to quarrel.
   d) When her mother came to kiss the children goodnight, why did Roberta pretend that she was asleep?
      Roberta didn't want her mother to know that she knew she had been crying.
   e) Why do you think that Mother didn't want to talk about where their father had gone?
      Mother didn't want to have to tell the children that their father had been arrested.
2. In your book write three interesting sentences about each of these characters:
   a) Ruth   b) Mother   c) Peter   d) Roberta
   Notes: *This calls for pupils to draw inferences, from the passage, about the characters, and to present these in a concise, summary form.*
3. In a few sentences, summarise the main idea of the passage.
   Notes: *This question calls for pupils to draw on clues from the text to infer the main idea of the passage and then present this in a concise, summary form.*

Now try these
figurative language; evaluation

1. The author uses some interesting phrases. Find these in the passage, and explain what they mean:
   a) 'He looks like the dead, Mum'
      Ruth thinks 'the master' looks very pale and shocked.
   b) The children heard boots go out and down the steps.
      The children couldn't be sure what was happening, but they knew there were footsteps.
   c) Her dear face was as white as her lace collar.
      When their mother, of whom the children were all very fond, came in she looked very shaken.
   d) Roberta lingered   *Roberta hung around, and let the others go ahead.*
   e) she lay mousy-still   *she lay totally still and quiet*
   f) she sank into an arm-chair   *Mother fell back exhausted into an armchair.*

2. This short section occurs near the beginning of the famous story of 'The railway children'. Did you enjoy the passage? Might you like to read the rest of the story? Give your reasons.
   Notes: *This calls for pupils to review the text and write persuasively about the judgements they make.*

Notes: *The Railway Children is an excellent book for reading aloud to the whole class. As well as encouraging a love for good literature, you can judiciously discuss aspects of the story, the plot, the setting and characterisation as seems appropriate – helping pupils with the development of their comprehension skills.*

Unit 10 Gulliver's Travels

Do you remember?
true/false/can't tell; literal answering in sentences

1. Write in your book 'true', 'false' or 'can't tell' for each of these statements.
   a) Gulliver was a sea captain.   *false*
   b) His ship was wrecked on its way to South America. *can't tell*
   c) It was close to midday when he awoke on the beach. *false*
   d) Gulliver counted about 400 little people.   *false*
   e) Gulliver realised that they were speaking Italian.   *false*
   f) He thought the place was called Lilliput as this was a name the little people used.   *true*
   g) The little people refused to feed Gulliver.   *false*
   h) Gulliver never did realise that he had been drugged by the little people.   *false*

2. *Pupils should write a sentence in their own words to answer each question.*
   a) How did the little people restrain Gulliver?
      The little people bound his hands, feet and his hair.
   b) What happened when Gulliver gave a great shout?
      When Gulliver shouted the little people all ran back in fright, and some fell off.
   c) Why did he decide it was better not to try to escape?
      He didn't want to make his captors more angry.
   d) What was Gulliver given to eat?
      Gulliver was given lamb, turkey and beef to eat.
   e) Why were the little people not worried about undoing some of his ropes?
      They knew he had been given a sleeping potion and so would soon be fast asleep.

More to think about
deductive answering in sentences; character empathy

1. Write a sentence to say how we can tell that:
   a) Gulliver woke early in the morning?
      The sun had just begun to rise above the horizon when he woke.
   b) the sheep and cattle on Lilliput were also very small?
      Three baskets of food scarcely made a mouthful for Gulliver.
   c) the little people were good cooks?
      Gulliver said that the food was deliciously cooked.

2. From what you can tell from the passage, write a few sentences describing the sort of person you imagine Gulliver to have been. Think particularly about his personality, and the way he reacted in a crisis.
   Notes: *This question calls for pupils to show empathy with Gulliver's character.*

Notes: *Many imaginative possibilities are suggested when pupils are encouraged to think themselves into situations of*

either being out of scale with their normal environment or stranded in a hostile place.

Now try these
vocabulary enrichment; summary; situation empathy

1. In the passage, find the following words. Write another word that could be used in place of each word without altering the meaning.
   a) astonishment *amazement/surprise*
   b) roared *shouted*   c) indicate *show*   d) peered *looked*
   e) violent *strong*   f) inhabitants *residents*

2. Write a brief summary, using no more than forty words, giving all the key facts of the passage.
   Notes: *Pupils need to identify the correct/main points in a concise way.*

3. Individually, the Lilliputians could not have restrained the huge outsider, but working together they did. Write about something you have achieved by working with other people that would have been impossible to do by yourself.
   Notes: *This question calls for pupils to show empathy in order to 'think themselves into' this situation, describing what happened.*

Progress Unit A

Do you remember?
cloze
Score: 1 mark for each correct answer (maximum 10 marks).
Pupils should note that the following words are missing.
1. *girl*   2. *cold*   3. *father*   4. *matches*   5. *home*   6. *light*
7. *flame*   8. *stove*   9. *feet*   10. *out*

More to think about
sequencing; deduction
Score: Q1 2 marks for a correct sequence, 1 mark if the sequence has one error; Q2a 3 marks (1 mark for each component); Q2b-f 1 mark per part; Q3 Up to 3 marks for a clear and concise description of the setting (maximum 13 marks).

1. The items should be sequenced as follows:
   an enormous iron stove with brass ornaments
   an enormous roast goose
   a Christmas tree with thousands of tiny, twinkling candles
   her grandmother

2. *Pupils should write a sentence in their own words to answer each question.*
   a) How can you tell that the little match girl's family were very poor?
      We can tell that the little girl's family were poor because she had to borrow her mother's slippers, her own house was very cold and in poor repair, and even in bad weather she needed to go out to sell matches.
   b) Why would her father have been cross had she gone home without selling the matches?
      He was probably very anxious that the family had no money for food.
   c) Did she usually light matches from the bundles? Explain the reason for your answer.
      No; the little girl was considering how wonderful it would be to light a match, implying that she had not done it before.
   d) What do you think caused the little girl to imagine such vivid scenes as she struck each match?
      The little girl was probably drifting into unconsciousness with the cold.

e) To which of her relations had the little girl felt particularly close?
   She was probably close to her grandmother.
f) Why did she have a smile on her lips when she was found dead?
   She was happy to be with her grandmother, and away from the terrible conditions and the cold.

3. Describe in your own words the place where the story of the little match girl is set.
   Notes: *This question calls for pupils to deduce from clues in the text what the place was like.*

Notes: *If you wish to, you can make a teaching point of the fact that language changes over time, pointing out that 'match girl' is hyphenated in the original text.*

Now try these
review; character empathy

Score: the marks awarded in this section are discretionary, according to your judgement. The pieces need not be awarded marks individually; what is significant is the extent to which the child is beginning to establish reasonable arguments and promote opinions, and use empathy to 'think themselves into' characters and situations and explore their feelings. For this reason an alternative to asking for all the questions to be completed is for the child to be allowed to select just one or two tasks, and for these to be worked on in more depth. Marks towards the higher end of the scale should be reserved for those presenting their work in well constructed and appropriately punctuated sentences (maximum 7 marks).

1. Did you enjoy this story by Hans Christian Andersen? Give your reasons.
2. The little match girl was frightened to go home.
   a) How do you think her parents were feeling when she didn't return?
   b) Do you think she was right to stay out?
3. Have you ever been afraid to admit to something you have done that you shouldn't, or something you haven't done that you should? Describe how you felt and what happened in the end.

Indicative scores for National Curriculum

Below level 3	Level 3	Level 4	Level 5
0-5	6-14	15-22	23-30

Indicative scores for 5–14 Guidelines

Below level C	Level C	Level D	Level E
0-9	10-15	16-26	27-30

Unit 11 A Smugglers' Song

Do you remember?
selecting the correct answer

Pupils should select the correct answer from two possible choices.

1. At what time do the horses go by?
   b) The horses go by at midnight.
2. How many ponies are used?
   a) 25 ponies are used.
3. What is hidden under the brushwood?
   b) Brandy-wine is hidden under the brushwood.

4. What are the colours of the uniforms of the King's men?
   b) The King's men wear blue and red uniforms.
5. How many dogs are kept to guard the house?
   b) There are two guard dogs.

More to think about
deductive answering in sentences

Pupils should write a sentence in their own words to answer each question.

1. Where do you imagine the story of this poem is set?
   The poem is set in a fishing village.
2. Who is the poem talking to? How can you tell whether they are male or female?
   The poem is talking to a young girl from the village, who is referred to as 'pretty maid'.
3. What is the person being told?
   She is being told to take no notice of the smugglers.
4. Who are 'the Gentlemen', and who are 'King George's men'?
   'The gentlemen' are the smugglers, and 'King George's men' are the soldiers.
5. Why do you think that the brandy-wine will be gone by the next day?
   The smuggled goods will be collected and taken away as soon as possible after being brought ashore.
6. Why is mother mending a coat with a wet lining?
   It is probably the coat of her husband (the child's father) torn while involved with the smuggling operation.
7. Whose dogs are Trusty and Pitcher? Why don't they bark?
   The dogs belong to the family, and don't bark because they recognise the smugglers.
8. What is meant by 'watch the wall' in this poem?
   In the poem, 'watch the wall' means don't look, and pretend you haven't seen anything.

Now try these
listing; deduction; empathy

1. Make a list of the items mentioned in the poem that have been smuggled.
   brandy; baccy (tobacco); laces; letters; doll
2. Is the poet on the side of the smugglers or King George's men? How can you tell?
   Pupils are being asked to deduce that the poet is on the smugglers' side because the poem is told sympathetically from the point of view of the smugglers. Pupils may answer that the poet is on the smugglers' side because he is telling the girl not to give them away.
3. Imagine that you lived in this little fishing village, several hundred years ago, and your father has asked you to join the smugglers tonight for the first time. Describe how you are feeling and what happens as you lead the horses down to the beach on this dark, still night.
   Notes: *This question calls for pupils to use empathy in order to 'think themselves into' this situation, and explore their feelings. This poem lends itself to dramatisation and choral speaking, and the whole theme of smugglers and smuggling (both in history and in the present day) is one that can excite pupils' imaginations and lead to related language work.*

Unit 12 The BFG

Do you remember?
literal answering in sentences

Pupils should write a sentence in their own words to answer each question.

1. Who wrote the story of the BFG?
   'The BFG' was written by Roald Dahl.
2. What do the initials BFG stand for?
   BFG stands for Big Friendly Giant.
3. Where was Sophie when the BFG found her?
   Sophie was in bed when the BFG found her.
4. What did she think he might do to her?
   At first Sophie was frightened that the BFG might eat her.
5. What did BFG have in his suitcase?
   The BFG had several empty glass jars in his suitcase.
6. What was he holding in his right hand?
   In his right hand he was holding a long net.
7. What was the first thing he caught?
   The first thing he caught was a winksquiffler.

More to think about
inference; deduction

Pupils should write a sentence in their own words to answer each question.

1. What sort of dream is a winksquiffler?
   A winksquiffler is a pleasant dream.
2. What is the difference between a winksquiffler and a phizzwizard?
   A phizzwizard is an even happier dream than a winksquiffler.
3. Why did the giant ask Sophie to 'kindly stop breathing'?
   He wanted Sophie to be totally silent to avoid frightening the dreams away.
4. What is a trogglehumper?
   A trogglehumper is a nightmare.
5. What was special about the particular trogglehumper the BFG caught?
   The trogglehumper that the BFG caught was a really bad nightmare, a bogthumper and a gobswitcher.
6. How did catching the trogglehumper affect the BFG?
   He was so upset that he didn't want to go on dream-hunting.
7. How can you tell that the giant was probably at least ten times bigger than Sophie?
   The BFG was so tall Sophie could sit in his waistcoat pocket.

Now try these
vocabulary development; empathy; appreciation

1. The BFG was sometimes confused by certain words and phrases. Write what he should have said instead of:
   a) I is not a cannybull. *I am not a cannibal.*
   b) little mices *little mice*
   c) This will be giving some little tottler a very happy night.
   This will be giving some little toddler a very happy night.
   d) what is I catching? *what am I catching?*
   e) This one would make your teeth stand on end.
   This one would make your hair stand on end.
   f) Oh, I is so glad I is clutching it tight.
   Oh, I am so glad I am clutching it tight.
   g) the poor little human-beaney tottlers
   the poor little human-being toddlers
2. In your book write what each of these people might say if the BFG appeared to them:
   a) your teacher, when BFG looks through the classroom window
   b) your mum, when you bring him home for tea

c) the bus driver, when he tries to squeeze onto his bus
d) the dentist, when he arrives at the surgery with a bad toothache
Notes: *This question calls for pupils to use empathy to think about these characters and their situations, and explore their feelings.*

3. What do you think would be the best things and worst things about being a giant? Make two lists.
   Notes: *This question calls for pupils to use what they know, from the passage, about the giant to 'think themselves into' his character and situation.*
4. If you were a story 'judge', how many marks out of 10 would you give the story of the BFG? Explain why you would award it this score.
   Notes: *This calls for pupils to show appreciation in the explanations they give, writing persuasively about their judgements. Selected children might be invited to offer their views on this and/or other pieces of writing to their group or to the whole class. In this way a culture of considering the merits or weaknesses of stories, poems, and non-fiction texts can begin to be encouraged.*

Unit 13 The King, Compere Lapin and Compere Tig

Do you remember?
matching questions and answers

Pupils are given a list of questions and a list of answers and are asked to match them.

1. At what time of day did the King visit his pool?
   The King visited his pool in the morning.
2. What was the weather like when the King went to the pool?
   It was warm and sunny when the King visited the pool.
3. Why was the King furious when he saw the pool?
   Someone had visited the pool before him and left it murky and dirty.
4. Why was Compere Tig arrested?
   Compere Tig was arrested because the King later saw him in the pool.
5. Who had told Compere Tig he could swim in the pool?
   Compere Lapin had told Compere Tig that the King had said he could bathe in the pool.

More to think about
literal answering in sentences

1. Pupils should write a sentence in their own words to answer each question.
   a) Who was responsible for making the King's pool 'murky and dirty'?
   Compere Lapin was responsible for making the King's pool 'murky and dirty'.
   b) Why did Compere Lapin want Compere Tig to bathe in the pool?
   He wanted Compere Tig to take the blame for the murky pool.
   c) How did he encourage Tig to go into the pool?
   He told Tig that the King had said that he may bathe in the pool.
   d) What was Tig's reaction when Lapin suggested that he might swim in the King's pool?
   Tig was flattered and delighted that the King should have given him permission to use the pool.
   e) 'Ou kai bwelay' is a phrase in the St Lucian dialect, that appears twice in the story. What might it mean?
   'that fooled you' (or similar)

2. Explain in your own words how Compere Tig persuaded Compere Lapin to change places with him.
3. Copy the words and phrases that the writer uses to encourage the reader to dislike Compere Lapin and to think he is a generally unpleasant character.
Compere Lapin visited Compere Tig to make fun of him; being a very greedy fellow

Now try these
evaluation; empathy; outcome prediction

1. Do you think Compere Lapin was fairly treated? Give your reasons.
This question calls for pupils to evaluate Compere Lapin's treatment, drawing on clues from the text.
2. At the end of the story it seems that Lapin is going to be very cruelly killed. Describe the sorts of feelings this makes you have for each of the characters?
This question calls for pupils to be empathetic towards Lapin's situation and to describe their feelings.
3. Make up your own ending for the story. Is Lapin killed, or is it a clever trick to frighten him, or even a trick to get him to marry the King's daughter? You may have other ideas. The King comes to talk to Compere Lapin as he swings, terrified, in the bag. Write the conversation that takes place.
Notes: *Pupils will use their knowledge of the characters and the story so far to predict this outcome.*
Notes: *This story can be used to stimulate oral work, either within a group or with the class as a whole. Themes such as 'whether two wrongs make a right' and betraying a friend can be explored.*

Unit 14 Looking Down

Do you remember?
sentence completion

Copy these sentences into your book about landing in this aeroplane at night. Write a sensible ending for each one.
1. As we come into land, there is a wonderful display of *twinkling lights.*
2. The ancient buildings can be seen because they are stretching up *towards us.*
3. In the darkness the traffic looks like *creatures with glowing eyes.*
4. The thing that it is difficult to see is probably a *river, lake or open space.*
5. Looking up I can see *stars and the moon.*

More to think about
deductive answering in sentences

1. *Pupils should write a sentence in their own words to answer each question.*
   a) Is the aeroplane landing late in the evening or early in the morning? How can you tell?
   b) What are the 'ribbons of orange' that stretch out 'into the sea of blackness'?
   c) What 'banishes the darkness from the city'?
   d) What are the creatures with glowing eyes?
   e) What is being described in the final paragraph?
2. Imagine that you are on an aeroplane, but coming into this busy city airport during the day. Describe what you can see.

Now try these
vocabulary enrichment

1. Which word in the passage means:
   a) a very large number *myriad*
   b) a place to shelter *haven*
   c) sending away *banishing*
   d) historic buildings *monuments*
   e) lighted up *glow, twinkling, shine, glowing, shimmering, neon*
2. From the way each of these words is used in the passage, say what you think it means.
   a) engulfing *covering*   b) frenetic *frantic*
   c) neon *coloured lights*   d) bulk *large*
   e) medley *mixture*   f) swathes *broad strips*
3. Look again at the six words in question 2. Use a thesaurus to find other words with similar meanings that the writer might have used. Copy them into your book.

Unit 15 Save It!

Do you remember?
selecting the correct answers

Pupils should select the right answer for each question from three possible choices.
1. How long have the water companies been given to prepare their plans?
   b) three weeks
2. What is to be their top priority?
   c) stopping leaks
3. Why might water meters be introduced?
   b) to encourage people to use less water
4. How much domestic water is used in toilets?
   b) a third
5. In what are we asked to collect rain water for the garden?
   a) a water butt
6. What shouldn't we use unless essential?
   c) a sprinkler

More to think about
summary; literal; deduction

1. Pretend you are the reporter who wrote this article. Your editor has said it is far too long, and you must rewrite it to about half its present length. This means you can use approximately 150 words, but you mustn't leave out any essential information.
2. *Pupils should write a sentence in their own words to answer each question.*
   a) Who has asked the water companies to prepare plans?
   The Government has asked the water companies to prepare plans.
   b) Why have they been asked to act urgently?
   They need to act urgently because there is a current water shortage.
   c) Why might it help if they offer to repair leaks on customers' land without charging?
   Customers are less likely to report leaks if they think they may need to pay for them being mended.
   d) Why are water meters unfair to families with several children?
   Families with several children need to use more water than other families.
3. Make lists of the ways you could save water:
   a) at school   b) at home
   Notes: *This question calls for pupils to draw on experience/knowledge outside the text.*

Now try these
establishing arguments

1. Prepare a design for a poster that is intended to promote one of the water saving tips.
2. We live in a country that usually has plenty of rainfall. Do you think we should be able to use as much water as we want whenever we want, or should we be 'more conservation minded'? Give reasons for your answer.

Notes: *These questions enable pupils to practise presenting persuasive and reasoned arguments. A useful extension can be to ask selected children to debate the merits of either water conservation or unrestricted availability of water.*

Unit 16 The Phantom Tollbooth

Do you remember?
cloze

Pupils should note that the following words are missing:
1. *forest* 2. *shoes* 3. *three* 4. *Christmas* 5. *family*
6. *air* 7. *head* 8. *adult* 9. *feet* 10. *ground*

More to think about
literal and deductive answering in sentences

1. Pupils should write a sentence in their own words to answer each question.
   a) What did Milo think was beautiful?
      Milo thought that the magical forest was beautiful.
   b) Why did the strange boy suggest some people might not find forests beautiful?
      He suggested that whether things seem beautiful depends on how you look at them.
   c) What fascinated Milo most about the strange boy?
      Milo was most fascinated by the fact that his feet did not touch the ground.
   d) Why did the boy assume Milo was older than he looked?
      The boy thought Milo was older because his feet already reached the ground.
   e) What did the boy think would be the main disadvantage of starting on the ground, and growing upwards?
      The main disadvantage of growing upwards is that things seem different as your head keeps changing its height.
2. From what you can tell from the passage, describe the characters of Milo and the strange boy. Do you think they are similar sorts of people, or are they very different? Which of the two would you have preferred to have as a friend? Give your reasons.
   Notes: *This question calls for pupils to deduce from clues in the text what each character is like.*

Notes: *This activity gives the opportunity to discuss the nature of friendships and to tackle issues of bullying and mutual respect in a non-threatening context.*

Now try these
empathy

1. Have you ever imagined what it would feel like to float in the air, just as we can float in water in a swimming pool or at the seaside?
   a) Make a list of the advantages the boy gives for being able to float above the ground.
      Your head remains at a constant height and so you see things from a constant angle.
      You don't hurt yourself when you fall over.
      You don't scuff your shoes.
      You don't mark the floor.

b) Make a list of any other advantages you can think of.
c) What would you most like to do if you could float in the air. Give your reasons.

Notes: *These questions call for pupils to use empathy to 'think themselves into' this situation, and explore their feelings.*

2. Many stories have been written, and many films made, where people are able to do things that are really impossible except in our fantasies. Write about your favourite 'fantasy' story, and say what it is about the story that you particularly like.

Notes: *This question asks pupils to enter into the story and think about how it makes them feel.*

Unit 17 The TV Kid

Do you remember?
true/false/can't tell

Read these sentences about the story. Write in your book 'true', 'false', or 'can't tell' for each one.
   1. Lennie's favourite occupation was watching television. *true*
   2. His mother always turned off the television while he was doing his homework. *false*
   3. Lennie's favourite programme was *Give It a Spin*. *can't tell*
   4. One day he was invited to be a contestant on *Give It a Spin*. *true (in his dream)*
   5. There were twenty all-expenses paid holidays on the Vacation Wheel. *true*
   6. There were also twenty zonk trips. *false*
   7. The worst zonk trip was to the haunted house. *can't tell*
   8. Lennie was pleased to have won his zonk trip. *false*
   9. He was told he could have a holiday to anywhere he chose if first he stayed in the haunted house. *false*
   10. Lennie asked if he could take the cash rather than the trip. *true*

More to think about
summary; deduction; outcome prediction

1. Rewrite the story in your own words, describing what happened, rather than writing it as a conversation.
   Notes: *This question calls for pupils to identify the main points correctly.*
2. Pupils should write a sentence in their own words to answer each question.
   a) What clues tell us that this is an American story?
      We can tell the story is American because the prize is in dollars, and some of the words used by the host of the game, such as 'merchandise', 'vacation', 'folks' and 'downtown' are more usual in America.
   b) Do you think that at first Lennie was pleased to be on the show?
      At first he was pleased to be on the show, but he changed his mind later.
   c) When and why did his attitude about the show change?
      He changed his mind when he won a zonk trip to a haunted house.
   d) What reasons made it difficult for him to turn down his zonk trip?
      He was embarrassed to turn down the zonk trip in front of such a big audience who might think he was a coward.
3. How do you think the story might have worked out? Write your own ending.
   Notes: *This question calls for pupils to think back over the story in order to predict the outcome.*

Now try these
empathy

1. Some of the most frightening stories and films are those that are almost believable.
   Pupils should write sentences in their own words to answer each question.
   a) How does the author make this into a rather frightening situation?
   b) How does it make you feel about the host of the programme?
   c) How do you feel for Lennie by the end of the passage?

2. Write about your worst nightmare. Explain why it was particularly frightening.
   Notes: *This question calls for pupils to use empathy to 'think themselves into' the situation of their nightmare, and to explore how it made them feel.*

Unit 18 Hiawatha's Childhood

Do you remember?
cloze from passage

1. The wigwam stood by the shores of *Gitchie Gumee*.
2. It was the wigwam belonging to *Nokomis*, Daughter of the Moon.
3. Behind it was a large *forest*, with many pine *trees*.
4. It was here that Nokomis nursed *Hiawatha*.
5. She called him her little *owlet*.
6. She showed him many things, including *Ishkoodah* the comet.
7. Nokomis also told him the story of the *warrior* who threw his *grandmother* at the moon.
8. Hiawatha called the birds his *chickens* and the animals his *brothers*.

More to think about
deductive answering in sentences

1. In your own words, write a detailed word picture of how you imagine the countryside and surroundings where Hiawatha grew up.
   Notes: *This question calls for pupils to deduce from clues in the text what the countryside was like.*

2. Pupils should write a sentence in their own words to answer each question.
   a) Do we know whether Nokomis was Hiawatha's mother?
      According to the poem, Nokomis was old and wrinkled and so was probably too old to be his mother.
   b) Who else could she have been?
      She could have been his grandmother or another elderly woman of the tribe who looked after the small children.
   c) How was Hiawatha's cradle constructed?
      Hiawatha's cradle was made of linden (lime tree) twigs, bound with reindeer sinews, and with moss and rushes for the bedding.
   d) Explain what the poet meant by 'Saw the moon rise from the water'.
      The moon came up from behind the lake, so would have appeared to have risen from the water.
   e) Why was it important for Hiawatha to learn about the natural world?
      When Hiawatha was young he would have needed to be able to hunt and gather food in the wild if he was to survive.

3. Nokomis taught Hiawatha about the sky at night, the stars, the constellations, the Milky Way and many other things.
   a) What was Ishkoodah   *a comet*
   b) What were its 'fiery tresses'?   *the tail*
   c) What was 'the Death-Dance of the spirits. Warriors with their plumes and war-clubs'?   *the Auroras Borealis or Northern Lights*
   d) What was 'the broad, white road in heaven, Pathway of the ghosts'?   *the Milky Way*

Now try these
use of rhythm; empathy

1. As you read this poem to yourself you will notice that it has a strong rhythm. Of what does it remind you?
   Native American dancing

2. From this poem it would seem that Hiawatha had an idyllic childhood. But there must have been many aspects of his life that were difficult and unpleasant. Make lists of the best and worst things about being a Native American child brought up in North America 150 years ago.
   Notes: *This question calls for pupils to draw on knowledge and experience from outside the text in order to 'think themselves into' the situation of a Native American child 150 years ago. Hiawatha is an excellent poem for choral speaking, and can be found in most major poetry anthologies.*

Notes: *If you wish to, you can make a teaching point of the fact that language changes over time, pointing out that 'pine trees' is hyphenated in the original text.*

Unit 19 Martin's Mice

Do you remember?
literal answering in sentences

Pupils should write a sentence in their own words to answer each question.

1. Why was Martin no ordinary kitten?
   Martin didn't like to chase mice.
2. What happened when he saw his first mouse?
   He caught it without thinking.
3. Where did he catch his first mouse?
   He caught his first mouse in the cart-shed loft.
4. What did Martin learn about collie-dogs?
   Martin learnt that collie-dogs chase cats.
5. Which of the humans made the biggest fuss of Martin?
   The farmer's daughter made the biggest fuss of Martin.

More to think about
inference and deduction; figurative language

1. Pupils should write sentences in their own words about each of the following.
   a) where Martin lived
   b) the humans who lived on the farm
   c) Martin's mother
   This question calls for pupils to draw inferences and make deductions from clues in the text.

2. Write a sentence to answer each of these questions.
   a) Why did Martin get confused about whether rabbits were pets or not?
      He was confused because some people eat rabbits.
   b) How do you think the saying 'curiosity killed the cat' first came about?
      Cats can put themselves into dangerous situations because they are natural explorers.

c) What is meant when the author says the mouse was 'rooted to the spot'?
'Rooted to the spot' means unable to move because of fear.

d) What did he think was the mouse's name? Why was this?
Martin thought the mouse's name was 'Pregnant' because she begged him to spare her life saying that she was pregnant.

Now try these
evaluation; prediction

1. Pretend you are judging a story writing competition. Score this passage from *Martin's Mice* by Dick King-Smith out of 10. Give the reasons for your decision, saying why you either liked or didn't like the extract. Use these headings, and give examples of:
   a) how well he develops the characters
   b) how clearly he describes the setting
   c) how cleverly the plot unfolds
   d) how much you are amused by the way he describes the situations.
   Notes: *This question calls for pupils to review the text, writing persuasively about their judgements.*

2. What do you think might happen next in the story? Plan the next chapter, then write it neatly in your book.

3. Describe what you think happened in the end.
   Notes: *Questions 2 and 3 require pupils to think back over the story in order to predict what might come next.*

Notes: *These questions provide a basic structure to enable the children to consider the books they read, and to evaluate them. Extend the activity by applying the model to another story or extract, perhaps one currently being read to or in the class.*

Unit 20   Deserts

Do you remember?
literal

1. Find the answer to each of these questions by looking at the map.
   a) Which is the biggest desert in Africa?
   Sahara Desert
   b) Name the deserts through which the Tropic of Capricorn passes.
   Atacama Desert, Kalahari Desert, Australian Desert
   c) What is the name of the desert in the centre of Asia?
   Gobi Desert
   d) Are there any major deserts in Europe?
   No
   e) Which large island, crossed by one of the tropics, is more than half desert?
   Australia

2. Find the answer to each of these questions by looking at the diagram.
   a) Over which ocean do the winds blow?
   Pacific Ocean
   b) Name the first range of mountains the winds cross.
   Coastal Mountains
   c) What happens in the San Joaquin Valley?
   most of the rain falls
   d) What is the second range of mountains called?
   Sierra Nevada Mountains
   e) When the winds have crossed these mountains, are they wet or dry?
   dry

More to think about
deductive answering in sentences

Pupils should write a sentence in their own words to answer each question.

1. Most people enjoy sunshine, so why do very few live in the deserts of the world?
   It is difficult to live in the deserts mainly because of the lack of water.

2. Why aren't there any major deserts in Europe?
   The winds blow across the Atlantic and carry plenty of moisture, and there aren't many mountains near the coast to stop the rain moving inland.

3. Is there a greater area of desert to the north or south of the Equator?
   There is rather more desert south of the Equator.

4. As the winds blow across the oceans, do they gain or lose moisture?
   Winds blowing across oceans usually gain moisture.

5. Looking at the diagram, describe why the winds are dry by the time they reach Death Valley.
   By the time the winds reach Death Valley they have already dropped most of their moisture on the two mountain ranges.

6. Why do you think Death Valley has that name?
   Death Valley was so named because it was such an inhospitable environment for the early settlers, being a desert. It was where many died when trying to reach the west coast of America.

Now try these
vocabulary enrichment; note-making; empathy

1. Which word or phrase in each list means the same as the word in bold type? Use a dictionary to help you.
   a) precipitation   *rain and snow*
   b) inhospitable   *unfriendly*
   c) vapour   *moisture in the air*
   d) ocean   *large sea*
   e) solar   *to do with the sun*

2. Use a reference book or an encyclopaedia, and make notes about any one of the deserts shown on the map.

3. Deserts are inhospitable places to live, and survival can be almost impossible. Imagine that you are in a small aircraft that crashes in a desert; the pilot and all three passengers survive. Describe what happens in your desperate struggle to reach safety.
   Notes: *This question requires pupils to use empathy to 'think themselves into' this situation and explore their feelings and imagination. Extension work can be developed by asking pupils to compare and contrast the information they can find in selected reference works (including electronic sources if available), and to evaluate the way the information is presented.*

Progress Unit B

Do you remember?
literal answering in sentences

Score: 1 mark for each correct answer (maximum 6 marks).

Pupils should select the correct answer from three possible choices.

1. How often were Bat and Bush-Rat seen together?
   a) most of the time

2. What did they do together each evening?
   b) cook and eat

3. What did Bat think of Bush-Rat?
   c) he hated him

4. Who found Bush-Rat's dead body?
   b) his wife
5. What did the chief do about the crime?
   b) tried to arrest Bat
6. Where did Bat hide?
   b) in a cave

More to think about
deductive answering in sentences; summary
Score: Q1 1 mark for each part; Q2 up to 5 marks for a well-constructed resumé (maximum 10 marks).

1. Pupils should write a sentence in their own words to answer each question.
   a) Why would Bush-Rat not have expected Bat to cause him harm?
      Bush-Rat thought that Bat was his friend.
   b) Which of the two creatures was the better cook?
      Bat was the better cook.
   c) Why did Bat need two pots to carry out his deadly plan?
      He needed to be able to climb into one pot, that was cool, without scalding himself.
   d) Why did the bush-rat fall for the bat's deadly scheme?
      The bush-rat wouldn't have been expecting a friend to pull such a deadly trick.
      Notes: *If you wish to, you can make a teaching point of the fact that 'bush rat' and 'bat' are not given initial capital letters here, explaining the reasons for this to pupils.*
   e) Why would it have been difficult to have found Bat in the cave?
      It was dark, and the bat kept very still high in the cave.
2. Write a summary of the story, including all the essential facts, using no more than six interesting sentences.
   Notes: *Pupils should correctly identify the main points and present them concisely.*

Now try these
evaluation; vocabulary enrichment
Score: Q1 up to 6 marks for a well presented and well punctuated answer; Q2 8 marks, 1 mark for each reasonable answer (maximum 14 marks).

1. Folk tales, like this one, apparently about animals, are really about people and how they behave. Write in your own words what this folk tale can teach us about how people can sometimes act towards one another.
   Notes: *This question calls for pupils to identify salient points from the passage, and write persuasively about the judgements they make.*
2. Pupils are given words under two headings: 'Words from the passage' and 'Words/phrases the writer could have used instead'. They are asked to use a dictionary to help them to match words of similar meaning. The first match has been made for them, as an example.
   identical *exactly the same*
   demeanour *outward behaviour*
   gorgeous *delicious*
   devious *cunning*
   naive *simple and trusting*
   fatal *deadly*
   distraught *deeply upset*
   venture *dare to go out*

Indicative scores for National Curriculum

Below level 3	Level 3	Level 4	Level 5
0-5	6-14	15-24	25-30

Indicative scores for 5–14 Guidelines

Below level C	Level C	Level D	Level E
0-9	10-15	16-26	27-30

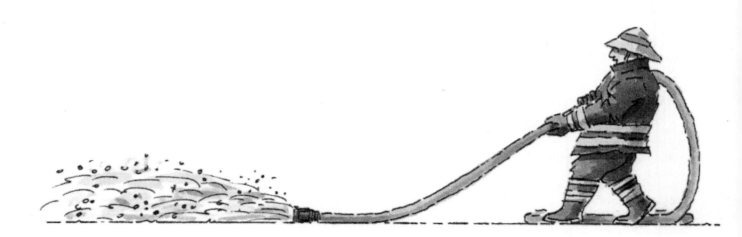